Celebrate Jesus!
AT CHRISTMAS

F O R   A D V E N T

T H R O U G H   E P I P H A N Y

Kimberly Ingalls Reese

CPH
SAINT LOUIS

This book is lovingly dedicated to my husband,
Dave, and our three children, Josiah, Samuel, and Sarah.
May we always celebrate Jesus at Christmas!

Copyright © 2000 Concordia Publishing House
3558 S. Jefferson Avenue, St. Louis, MO 63118-3968
Manufactured in the United States of America

Library of Congress Cataloging-in-Publication Data

Reese, Kimberly Ingalls, 1960-
    Celebrate Jesus! at Christmas : family devotions for Advent through Epiphany / Kimberly Ingalls Reese.
      pm. cm.
    ISBN 0-570--07127
    1. Advent—Prayer books and devotions—English. 2. Christmas—Prayer books and devotions—English. 3. Family—Prayer books and devotions—English. I. Title.
    BV40 .R44 2000

1   2   3   4   5   6   7   8   9   10   09 08 07 06 05 04 03 02 01 00

Table of Contents

These Devotions Are for You

*D*oes the flurry of activity in your family's celebrations blur the worship of Jesus? Does your awareness of Jesus' love for you fall to the wayside by the second week of December? Has Jesus been misplaced in all of the tinsel? Each year it seems we scurry here and there, packing more and more activities into the month of Christ's birth. In so doing our celebrations become more stressful than joyful.

One trap that befalls today's busy families is trying to do *too much too fast*. We feel we have to cut down the tree, set it up, decorate it and the entire house—all on the Friday after Thanksgiving! We fill every available inch of our calendar with activities, parties, and programs, leaving little time for quiet reflection.

Another trap is the unspoken belief that, as parents, we must make Christmas as magical as possible for our children. Very often the scurry and scramble for that elusive magic takes on a life of its own and creates expectations beyond reach. Actually, children have lower expectations than we think and are quite often satisfied with simplicity. Remember the year your two-year-old tossed aside that expensive toy and contentedly played with the box?

Often the level of excitement reaches fever pitch by mid-December, only for Christmas day to become anticlimactic—an empty room strewn with wrapping paper. Try slowing the pace, making Advent the focus of your Christmas holiday. *Fix your eyes on Jesus; who He is and who we are in Him.*

Savor this special season. Give your children a taste of excitement each day by involving them in the preparations—sending cards, decorating, baking, and giving gifts. Cultivate a yearning to know Jesus more. While things will not be done perfectly, you will be building precious memories to last a lifetime.

Celebrate Jesus! at Christmas is designed to help your busy family focus on the real meaning of Christmas; quieting your hearts and redirecting your minds to celebrate the coming of Christ. As we center our celebration around Him, it becomes easier to avoid the harried, commercial side of this sacred holiday, maintaining more of our normal routines. Jesus said, "Come to Me, all you who are weary and burdened, and I will give you rest" (Matthew 11:28).

As you read each devotion, experience the sense of anticipation and expectation as the Christmas story unfolds. Look to Jesus. Celebrate His birth. Seek Him in all you do, and the Holy Spirit will help you focus on Jesus with thanksgiving for God's promises and a renewed awareness of His continual presence and saving work in your lives—bringing you joy, peace, and love.

Tips for Making the Most of Your Time

Advent begins the fourth Sunday before Christmas. Make it special for your family by setting aside time for daily devotions. Gather in a favorite room where everyone is comfortable. Each devotion is approximately 15 minutes and can be done at any time of day when the family is gathered together.

The devotions are organized into the four weeks of Advent, as well as Christmas Eve, Christmas day, and the twelve days until Epiphany. Each devotion is divided into five simple parts—candle lighting, singing, listening to the lesson, praying, and nativity building.

Familiarize yourself with each devotion. A list of materials needed appears at the beginning of each week. If at all possible, prepare early—looking ahead and gathering the necessary materials into one box before the season of Advent even begins. Checking things out before each devotion will also help you avoid the last-minute scramble!

Remember that these are *family* devotions. Everyone can participate by lighting candles, reading, praying, singing, and putting the nativity figures in place. As each one participates, the message becomes more meaningful. Give everyone the opportunity to lead a devotion. You'll be surprised how quickly a fidgety child can become an excited leader. Even the youngest family member can express praise for God and all He has done for us through Jesus.

Sing! is the time for your family to praise the Lord as simply or as exuberantly as desired. Give children learning to play an instrument an opportunity to accompany the singing or play a solo. Often our own family's singing has dissolved into laughter upon hearing our joyful noises before the Lord. God takes pleasure in the songs of His people.

If your family is uncomfortable singing, read the songs out loud. Families with young children may want to limit the songs to one or two verses.

Lighting the candles is an important part of each devotion as it helps us recall that Jesus is the Light of the world. He brought His light into a cold, sinful, hurting world to provide love, healing, and salvation. Because of His death and resurrection, His light sparks a light within our souls. The candles also provide a visual for marking the passage of time until Christmas—creeping ever closer as more candles are lit.

Let older children light the candles and younger ones extinguish them. Name the candles as they are lit. Your Advent wreath will grow in beauty throughout Advent until at last on Christmas day it is all aglow, reflecting the love of Jesus.

A word of caution: Take caution with open flames. They can and do start fires. Do not leave your children unattended when the candles are lit.

Reading provides an opportunity to hear passages from the Bible read out loud. Vary the way each is read. Go around the circle one night, letting each family member read one verse. On another night, take turns reading the passage from different translations. Yet another suggestion is to read each one dramatically, like a play.

Make it exciting to hear God's Word. It is the embodiment of God's promise to us. Hearing the Word spoken aloud helps it take on new meaning. Talk about each passage as it is read; making sure everyone understands its meaning before going on to the next section.

Think about It provides questions and answers to use as a springboard for family discussions. Keep the ages of your children in mind, adapting the questions and answers to match the levels of understanding.

Nativity Building is an interactive way for the Christmas story to be written on your hearts. Individual pieces are gradually added to the manger scene as Christmas Eve approaches. Specific figures and directions are suggested each time.

If at all possible, gather all the materials for the building the nativity well in advance. Consider investing in a sturdy set of nativity figurines that can be used time and again.

Let's Pray offers a prayer upon which your family can expand, personalizing it to fit your family's individual needs and circumstances. Encourage your children to be involved in the prayers. Even the youngest child can offer their praise and love to Jesus through prayer.

Let's Live It is full of practical applications, offering suggestions for application of what your family has learned. Scripture tells us to teach God's truth to our children diligently, to talk of it when we sit in our homes, when we walk by the way, when we lie down, and when we rise up. We are to write His words on our doorposts and bind them on our hearts so that everyone can see by our lives that we know God (Deuteronomy 6:7–8 and Proverbs 3:3).

Ask for God's help in finding ways to accomplish this. Ideas include explaining the spiritual meaning of sending Christmas cards (extending "the Good News" greetings brought by the angels), helping elderly relatives in some of their holiday preparations, or driving a neighbor to see Christmas lights (reinforcing that Jesus is the Light of the world). Each activity is an opportunity to celebrate Jesus.

Consider the traditions your family already enjoys. Do any of them tie into the weekly themes? Spaces are provided at the end of each section for adding your own activities. Be creative! Don't miss any opportunity to write His message on the tablets of your heart. Ask God to oversee and design your Advent season—then stand back and watch Him at work. Be prepared for a sweet surprise!

Kimberly Ingalls Reese

Making Your Advent Wreath

Your family Advent wreath can be as simple or elaborate as desired. Its basic design is four tapered candles placed around a metal or ceramic candle holder shaped in a circle. A pillar candle is placed in the center.

A simple way to make a wreath is to insert four candles into a Styrofoam ring. If completely rounded, slice the ring in half lengthwise so that one side is flat. Gently work the four tapered candles into the Styrofoam. Add a drop of glue into the bottom of each hole to secure the candles. Decorate your wreath with greenery, using a green pipe cleaner to anchor the branches to the Styrofoam. Check the candles before the first devotion. They have a way of not staying in place the first time around!

The four candles around the outer ring can either be three purple and one pink, or four blue. Check with your pastor to see which set your church uses during Advent. It is best to match the colors used at home with those used in church.

The colors of the outer ring symbolize the royalty of Christ as king. Use a large, white pillar candle to place inside the circle, representing that Jesus was pure and without sin. The seasonal greenery surrounding the wreath reminds us of God's everlasting love—without beginning or end.

Display your wreath in a prominent place in your home, at the center of your holiday celebrations. Let it be the first decoration to go up and one of the last to come down. Before our own home was blessed with curious toddlers and preschoolers, we enjoyed having the wreath as our table's centerpiece. In recent years it has been equally appreciated on the living room mantle.

Advent is a solemn time: a time of waiting, of reflecting, and of repenting; a time set aside to prepare our hearts to celebrate the anniversary of Jesus' birth and to look forward to His second coming. Advent is followed by the celebration of Christmas which is then followed by the season of Epiphany, the afterglow carrying us into another year of service for our Lord and Savior, Jesus Christ.

As you and your family embark on this celebration of Jesus, may your hearts be filled with this early Christian blessing:

Praise God, who sends us the light of heaven!

May His light always light your path.

God Never Makes a Promise He Doesn't Keep!

But when the time had fully come, God sent His Son,

born of a woman, born under law, to redeem those under law,

that we might receive the full rights of sons. Galatians 4:4

Materials Needed This Week

Advent wreath with candles

Greens to surround the wreath

Matches

Holy Bible

A ring to leave at stable

A promise—parents, be ready to make a promise

Here we are at the beginning of Advent—a time of preparing our hearts to receive the greatest gift ever given. The word *advent* literally means coming: Jesus coming to earth as a babe; Jesus coming into our hearts as our Savior; Jesus coming again as King.

Christmas is meant to be a time of promise, reflection, repentance, expectation, giving, and great joy. During this first week of Advent we'll learn about God's promises to us. His written word, the Bible, is full of His promises to us and for our lives. God promised to send Jesus a long time before He came. Jesus came into this world to fulfill that promise.

Let's Live It

As your family begins preparing for Christmas, allow the promise theme to permeate your plans and set the tone for your celebration. Take opportunities to remind your children of these promises: Jesus is alive; He loves you—He is the fulfillment of God's promise.

1. Make a promise to your children that you will be able to keep during this week. This will help them experience the anticipation and joy of fulfillment. You could promise to make Christmas cookies together, to go Christmas shopping, or to play a special game as a family.

2. Look for Christmas lights in your neighborhood. Discuss how Jesus is the true light, the Light of the world.

3. Take a pajama drive one evening to look at the lights. Or weather permitting, take an evening walk around the block. Look for lighted crosses or stars that carry the true meaning of Christmas.

4. Each evening at dinner, pray that the promise of Jesus be real in the lives of those whose Christmas cards your family received that day. Make this a dinnertime practice throughout the season.

5.

6.

Sunday of the First Week

Lighting

Light the first purple (or blue) candle. This candle is called the *Promise Candle*. It helps us remember the promises God makes to us, His children.

Reading

Hebrews 6:12–19

Think about It

Promises are important to God—He never breaks a promise. We find God's promises to us throughout the Bible. They are an anchor for our souls, firm and secure. The Bible says that God promises to stay in 'an everlasting covenant' with us. That means God's promises will last forever (Psalm 89:3-4; Luke 1:68-80; Hebrews 9:11-28).

Jesus is the answer to God's most important promise—the promise to send a Savior.

Jesus is God's perfect Son who died and rose again to conquer sin.

What is a promise? What does it mean to make a covenant promise? A promise is a pledge or an oath to do something for someone else, no matter what. A covenant promise is an agreement between two people—it is a pledge from one person to another. Each says to the other "I will do it, no matter what!" It is believing something will happen even before it does.

Have you ever had to wait for a promise to come true? Was it worth it? God's people waited a long time for some of God's promises to be fulfilled. The prophet Isaiah told God's people that He would someday send a Savior to them (Isaiah 9:6-7). Isaiah taught about Jesus hundreds of years before the Savior actually came to earth. God's people looked forward to seeing the answer to that promise year after year, until it finally happened.

Can you talk about a time it was hard for you to keep a promise? Why is it important to keep our promises? The Bible warns against making oaths or promises that we cannot or do not want to keep. God wants us to be like Him, dependable and faithful in our promises. We thank God for His forgiveness each time we fail and we ask for God's help and wisdom in knowing how to keep our promises to each other.

What is your favorite promise from God? What makes it special to you? Let's look at some of God's promises. In Genesis 9:11-14, we discover that the rainbow is a sign of God's promise to never again flood the whole earth. In Galatians 4:4-7, we read that God promised to send His Son Jesus to be our Savior. John 17:2-3 tells us about His promise to give believers in Jesus eternal life. Jesus Himself promised to never leave us in Matthew 28:20.

Let's Pray

Dear God, thank You for being true to Your promise to send a Savior. Your love is so great! Help us draw closer to Jesus this holiday season and trust in the faithfulness of Your promises to us. We also pray for friends and family who do not know Jesus as their Savior (name them individually). Help them see the saving love of Jesus in the midst of their festivities. Amen.

Sing!

What a Friend We Have in Jesus

Joseph Scriven, 1820–86

CONVERSE
Charles C. Converse, 1832–1918

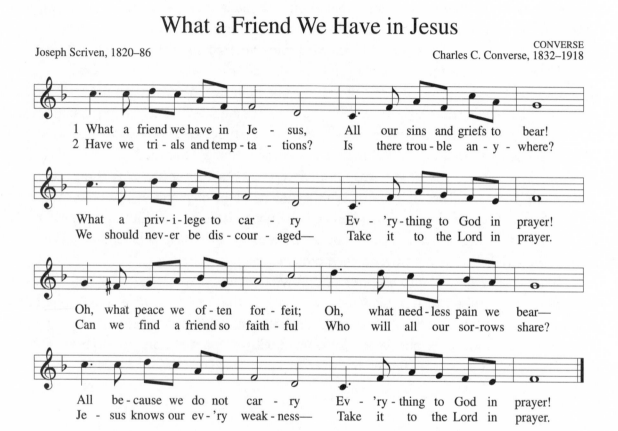

1 What a friend we have in Je - sus, All our sins and griefs to bear!
2 Have we tri - als and temp - ta - tions? Is there trou - ble an - y - where?

What a priv - i - lege to car - ry Ev - 'ry - thing to God in prayer!
We should nev - er be dis - cour - aged— Take it to the Lord in prayer.

Oh, what peace we of - ten for - feit; Oh, what need - less pain we bear—
Can we find a friend so faith - ful Who will all our sor - rows share?

All be - cause we do not car - ry Ev - 'ry - thing to God in prayer!
Je - sus knows our ev - 'ry weak - ness— Take it to the Lord in prayer.

Nativity Building

Begin to set up your nativity. Start by putting up the stable and empty manger. The empty manger helps us anticipate the fulfillment of God's promise.

Monday of the First Week

Lighting

Light the first purple (or blue) candle.
Ask the children to name the candle.

Reading

Genesis 2:21–25

Sing!

God Is So Good

Anonymous

Anonymous

1 God   is   so   good,   God   is   so   good,
2 I   praise   His   name,   I   praise   His   name,
3 He   an - swers   prayer,   He   an - swers   prayer,

God   is   so   good,   He's   so   good   to   me.
I   praise   His   name,   He's   so   good   to   me.
He   an - swers   prayer,   He's   so   good   to   me.

Think about It

Adam and Eve were the first people to promise to love each other in marriage. From then on they would be a team. The marriage relationship is a very important relationship between two people. Only our relationship with God is more important.

When people get married, they exchange wedding rings as a reminder of their covenant promise. The circle stands for the lifelong promise to love each other. God has made a lifelong promise to love us. Because of His great love for us, we want to give Him our love and commitment.

The wedding ring reminds us of the promises made when two people get married. What reminds us of the promise of Jesus' love for us? Baptism, the Lord's Supper, and the Word of God are reminders of His great love, shown to us through Jesus.

Let's Pray

Dear Jesus, thank You for Your great love, a love that will last forever. Help us to love, honor, and serve You each day. Make our hearts ready to receive You as Savior once again this Christmas season. Amen.

* Remember to pray for friends and relatives who do not yet know the wonderful love of Jesus. Be their light so that they might see the love of Christ in you.

Nativity Building

Place a ring in the stable as a reminder of our relationship with Jesus. We are eternally bound together in love.

Tuesday of the First Week

Lighting

Light the Promise Candle.

Reading

Isaiah 9:2, 6–7

Think about It

Hundreds of years before Jesus was born, Isaiah told people about His birth. Isaiah was a prophet who shared God's message with His people. God's words to Isaiah are in the Bible and we can still read them today.

What was Isaiah's message? Whom was God going to send? God promised to send His Son, who would be our Savior, a light in a world dark with sin. Isaiah calls Him Wonderful Counselor, Mighty God, Everlasting Father, Prince of Peace.

In Isaiah 42:6–7, God calls Jesus a covenant. In Old Testament times people entered into a covenant when they made an agreement to help each other. Two people made a pledge to each other by exchanging something of value such as a cloak, a staff, or a ring. Today we make commitments by exchanging rings in marriage, by shaking hands, or by signing a paper. The pledge shows you are serious about your commitment.

How is Jesus the covenant pledge to God's promise? We are sinners, and God knew that we would never be able to live a perfect life. So He sent Jesus to pay the price for our sins (John 3:16; 1 Corinthians 15:3). God kept His covenant promise through Jesus' death and resurrection. Because of Jesus, all believers will live eternally in heaven. God always keeps His promises.

Sing!

Oh, Come, All Ye Faithful

John F. Wade, c. 1711–86; tr. composite

ADESTE FIDELES
John F. Wade, c. 1711–86

1 Oh, come, all ye faith - ful, Joy - ful and tri - um - phant! Oh,
2 Sing, choirs of an - gels, Sing in ex - ul - ta - tion,

come ye, oh, come . . . ye to Beth - le - hem;
Sing, all ye cit - i - zens of heav - en a - bove!

Come and be - hold Him Born the king of an - gels:
Glo - ry to God . . . . . In . . . the . . . high - est:

Refrain

Oh, come, let us a - dore Him, Oh, come, let us a - dore Him,

Oh, come, let us a - dore Him, Christ the Lord!

Let's Pray

Dear God, thank You for sharing Your promise of a Savior through the words of Isaiah. You made a covenant with Your people that you fulfilled through Jesus. Help us to show our thanks by loving, honoring, and serving You. In Jesus' name. Amen.

Nativity Building

Place the figures of Mary and Joseph somewhere in the room, away from the stable. They will be moved closer and closer, reminding the children of Mary and Joseph's long journey to Bethlehem.

Wednesday of the First Week

Lighting

The shape of the Advent wreath is a circle with no beginning or end. It reminds us that God's love for us will never end. The evergreens in the wreath also remind us of God's everlasting love. They do not turn colors and fall off like other leaves; instead they stay green and remind us that God's love will never fail. Light the Promise Candle.

Reading

John 8:12

Sing!

This Little Gospel Light of Mine

Traditional   Traditional

1 This lit-tle Gos - pel light of mine, I'm going to let it shine;
2 All a - round___the neigh-bor-hood I'm going to let it shine;
3 Hide it___ un - der a bush-el? No! I'm going to let it shine;

This lit - tle Gos - pel light of mine, I'm going to let it shine;
All a - round___ the neigh-bor-hood I'm going to let it shine;
Hide it___ un - der a bush - el? No! I'm going to let it shine;

This lit - tle Gos - pel light of mine, I'm going to let it shine,
All a - round___ the neigh-bor-hood I'm going to let it shine,
Hide it___ un - der a bush - el? No! I'm going to let it shine,

Let it shine all the time, Let it shine.
Let it shine all the time, Let it shine.
Let it shine all the time, Let it shine.

22

Think about It

God promised to bring light into a world that was dark in sin. He kept that promise by sending Jesus. In John 8:12, Jesus called Himself the Light of the world. The candle that has been lit on our wreath symbolizes the light of Jesus. Just as light helps us see things around us, Jesus helps us see God's love and forgiveness.

Have you ever tried walking in the dark? Did you get very far without a light? If we walk in the dark, we cannot see and we may bump into things or even fall down. Walking without light is very difficult. Walking without the light of Jesus will only lead us into more darkness.

How are lighthouses and Jesus the same? Lighthouses warn ships of dangerous rocks ahead. Their flashing lights protect the ships from trouble. Jesus is the Light of the world (John 8:12), shining light into the darkness of sin. When we stop to look at our own sin, Jesus' light shows us the way to God's forgiveness and love through His death and resurrection.

Turn all the lights off in the room and leave only the one candle lit as you pray. Notice how that one small candle creates a welcoming glow, drawing you in and pointing you toward Jesus, the one true light.

Let's Pray

Thank You, Jesus, for being the Light of the world, our one true light. Forgive our sins and let the light of Your love shine through us this Christmas. When we see the candles of our Advent wreath and the twinkling lights on our Christmas tree, help us to remember the light of Your love. Amen.

Nativity Building

Life goes on as usual. All looks normal, yet the stage is being prepared. Place the animals in or near the stable. Jesus is coming.

Thursday of the First Week

Lighting

Continue to light only the Promise Candle. Talk about Jesus as the one true light.

Reading

1 John 1:5–10

Think about It

The gift of God's grace is amazing. As God looks down upon His creation, He is filled with compassion, love, and joy. So much so that He sent Jesus to share His love with us and to light our path back to Him.

Out of all the many promises God makes to us in the Bible, which is most precious? It is the promise of Jesus as Savior. God's Son has come to free us from sin and give us new life.

The Bible says that all who believe in Jesus will be saved—saved from what? We will be saved from eternal punishment for sin and the loneliness of being separated from God's love. By ourselves, we could never deserve God's love and forgiveness. But because Jesus died for us, God's grace and love are poured down upon us.

How do we know that God will forgive the wrong things we have done? We know that this is God's marvelous promise to us—whether we are four or eighty-four years old—because the Bible tells us so. In 1 John 1:9 we read that "If we confess our sins, [God] is faithful and just and will forgive us our sins." It is His Christmas gift to us.

24

Sing!

Amazing Grace

NEW BRITAIN

John Newton, 1725–1807, alt.

J. Carrell and D. Clayton, *Virginia Harmony*, 1831

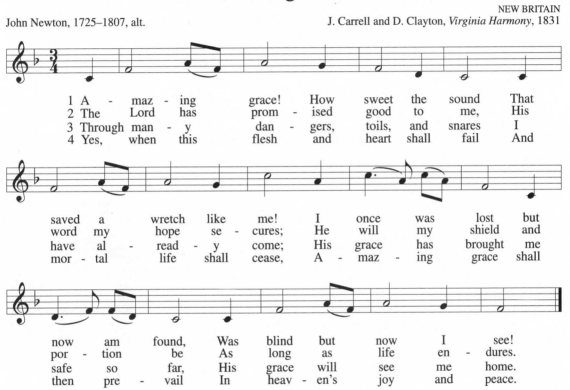

1 A - maz - ing grace! How sweet the sound That
2 The Lord has prom - ised good to me, His
3 Through man - y dan - gers, toils, and snares I
4 Yes, when this flesh and heart shall fail And

saved a wretch like me! I once was lost but
word my hope se - cures; He will my shield and
have al - read - y come; His grace has brought me
mor - tal life shall cease, A - maz - ing grace shall

now am found, Was blind but now I see!
por - tion be As long as life en - dures.
safe so far, His grace will see me home.
then pre - vail In heav - en's joy and peace.

25

Let's Pray

> Dear Lord, forgive me for the wrong things I have done today that have turned me away from Your light. I believe that You are my Savior. Give me Your strength to turn away from sin. Thank You for Your forgiveness today and every day. Amen.

Nativity Building

Place the shepherds some distance away from the stable and from Mary and Joseph. Remember that the shepherds were outside Bethlehem, tending sheep in their fields until the angels spoke to them. They had no idea what was about to happen.

Friday of the First Week

Lighting

Light the Promise Candle. Do you remember what the wreath stands for? The circle of candles and evergreens symbolize the eternal nature of God and His love that lasts forever.

Reading

John 14:1–6, 27

Sing!

Let Us Ever Walk with Jesus

Sigismund von Birken, 1626–81
Tr. *Lutheran Book of Worship*, 1978, alt.

LASSET UNS MIT JESU ZIEHEN
Georg G. Boltze, 1788

1 Let us ev - er walk with Je - sus, Fol - low His ex - am - ple pure,
2 Let us suf - fer here with Je - sus And with pa - tience bear our cross.

Through a world that would de - ceive us And to sin our spir - its lure.
Joy will fol - low all our sad - ness; Where He is, there is no loss.

On - ward in His foot - steps tread - ing, Pil - grims here, our home a - bove,
Though to - day we sow no laugh - ter, We shall reap ce - les - tial joy;

Full of faith and hope and love, Let us do our Fa - ther's bid - ding,
All dis - com - forts that an - noy Shall give way to mirth here - af - ter.

Faith - ful Lord, with me a - bide; I shall fol - low where You guide.
Je - sus, here I share Your woe; Help me there Your joy to know.

Think about It

Jesus returned to heaven after He finished His ministry on earth. Before He left, Jesus made a promise to His disciples. He told them that He was going to prepare a place for them in heaven. Their hope for a future in heaven was secure. Our hope is also secure in Jesus. We do not need to be afraid or troubled about anything, because Jesus has taken care of our biggest problem—sin—and has a special place waiting for us in heaven.

What did Jesus promise to do? He promised to make a special place for us with Him in heaven. Not only does Jesus give us forgiveness from our sins and grace for living every day, He also gives us everlasting life.

How do you think the promise of Jesus encouraged His disciples to live? It encouraged them to live in faith. We too can live in faith. We know that Jesus keeps His promises and that we can trust God with everything in our lives. We can trust that He is the source of peace and not worry or be afraid. Jesus is bigger than any problem we have and He will help us, no matter what.

Do we have to do anything to earn the peace that Jesus promised? No. The peace of Jesus is free to all who trust in Him. His peace is like a deposit—a small part of the promise of heaven. When an adult buys something big like a new car, he pays a small amount of money as a deposit. The money shows that he is going to do what he said: buy the car. When Jesus sends His peace to us, it gives us a small picture of the peace and joy that will be ours forever in heaven.

What will heaven be like? In Revelation 21:3, we read that God will live with His believers in heaven. We will see Him and be with Him. In fact, we won't need any kind of light because there will be no darkness in heaven—God will be our Light (Revelation 22:5). It is a wonderful place of happiness and joy. There is no crying, pain, sickness, or dying (Revelation 21:4). Best of all, we will live there forever with Jesus.

Let's Pray

Dear Jesus, help us to give all of our worries and fears to You. Send us Your peace and help us to trust in Your everlasting love. Thank You for the gift of heaven through Your death and resurrection. Amen.

Nativity Building

Place the Wise Men in a group away from the stable and all other figurines. Do not move them again until after Christmas. Their long journey did not begin until after the star shone over Bethlehem announcing Jesus' birth.

God's Angels Complete His Mission

Do not forget to entertain strangers, for by so doing

some people have entertained angels without knowing it.

Hebrews 13:2

Materials Needed This Week

Holy Bible

Advent wreath with candles

A wrapped ornament for each family member

Angels for the nativity

Matches

From the very beginning, God has communicated with us in many different ways. Adam and Eve, Noah, Moses, and others talked directly with God. Prophets and priests like Samuel, Isaiah, and Elijah received God's word and preached it to the people. God also sent angels to communicate His message to certain people. Today He talks to us through His written word, the Holy Bible.

God is constantly at work in our daily lives, strengthening our faith and keeping us close to Him. He provides everything we need, such as food and clothing, a home, family, and friends. He took care of our greatest need when He sent the Savior whose birth we celebrate at Christmas—Jesus, His own Son. God announced the birth of His Son in some miraculous, life-changing ways. He used angels as His messengers not once, not twice, but four times to deliver this important message.

First, the angel Gabriel appeared to Mary to tell her that she had been chosen to be the mother of the Messiah. Second, an angel appeared to Joseph in a dream telling him not to be afraid to marry Mary. The child she was carrying would be special—the Savior of the world.

Then an angel appeared to the shepherds and announced Jesus' birth, directing them to the manger where they would find the newborn King. Finally, after the Wise Men had visited the child Jesus, an angel warned Joseph to move his young family and leave for Egypt to avoid King Herod who was planning to kill the babies of Bethlehem.

Let's Live It

This week emphasize the various ways that God speaks to us. Encourage each other to listen to His Word and to talk to God in prayer. We communicate often with people we like, and especially with people we love. Discover new ways to communicate with one another and with God this week.

1. Ask each person to think of two different ways to creatively communicate with others in the family (i.e., talk together in a quiet spot, tuck a note in a lunch box or briefcase, or write a message in the snow). Be creative, just as God is creative in talking to us. (Adults, you may have to help younger children.)

2. Share your own proclamation of Jesus' birth. Send your Christmas cards this week. Ask your children to help choose the cards and include messages that share the Good News that Jesus, the Savior of the world, has been born. Explain to your children that the cards and their message are like the greetings the angel gave to Mary and Joseph.

3. Practice being "an angel" to others. As a family, do an anonymous good deed for someone else (i.e., shoveling a neighbor's driveway, baking cookies for an older adult, mowing a lawn, giving some flowers, or donating clothing or presents to a shelter). If you prefer to avoid the secrecy, simply help an older relative or neighbor with their holiday preparations, or sing Christmas carols at a nursing home or hospital.

4. Donate a gift for a child in need. Purchase a new toy, book, or clothing and donate the gift to a local organization or shelter. Or ask your children to choose one of their own "nearly new" toys to give. You may be surprised by what they choose. They might very well choose an expensive toy or even a highly prized one. Respect and encourage their sacrificial giving. (If you have already given gifts before reading this devotion, remind your children of your donation. Pray that the gift will bring God's joy to the child receiving it.)

5. Donate a Christian book or video that tells the Christmas story to your local library.

6.

7.

Saturday/Sunday of the Second Week

Lighting

Light the Promise Candle and the second purple (or blue) candle. The second candle is called the Angel Candle.

Reading

Matthew 18:10 and Hebrews 1:14

Think about It

The Bible tells us that God spoke to Mary, Joseph, and the shepherds in a very special way. He sent angels to bring some great news to them. These angel messengers told Mary, Joseph, and the shepherds about Jesus, the Savior of the world. This may seem surprising to us but that's how God decided to do it. As a family, discuss the following question and answers about angels.

God's angels are spiritual beings created to serve Him. What does this mean? The Bible tells us that angels worship God in front of His throne day and night. See Isaiah 6:1–4.

How do angels serve God? See Zechariah 1:10–11 to discover one thing angels do for God. In what other ways do angels serve God? God sends them to guide, protect, and comfort us. Angels are at work for us in many ways that we cannot see.

According to the Bible, angels are wise and know the difference between good and evil (2 Samuel 14:17). Can you name some Bible stories about angels? Remember Lot's rescue from Sodom and Gomorrah; Daniel and the lions; the three men in the fiery furnace; Jesus' resurrection and ascension into heaven. God's angels are real superheroes!

The good news is that God's angels are still at work today. The Bible says that God has given angels the special job of watching over us. Jesus' words in Matthew 18:10 suggest that God sends "guardian angels" to watch over all His children. (See also Psalm 34:7, Psalm 91:11, and Hebrews 1:14.) How does it feel to know that God has angels that are always watching out for you?

Let's Pray

Dear God, thank You for sending your angels to proclaim Your messages to people—especially the Good News about Jesus, our Savior from sin. When we are scared, help us remember that You are always with us and that You have sent Your angels to protect us. For Jesus' sake. Amen.

Nativity Building

Place an angel away from the nativity, in a place by itself. Discuss how God's angels are all around us, even though we cannot see them.

Sing!

Hark! The Herald Angels Sing

MENDELSSOHN

Charles Wesley, 1707–88, alt.

Felix Mendelssohn, 1809–47

1 Hark! The her - ald an - gels sing, "Glo - ry to the new-born king;
2 Christ, by high - est heav'n a - dored, Christ, the ev - er - last - ing Lord,
3 Hail the heav'n-born Prince of Peace! Hail the sun of righ-teous-ness!

Peace on earth and mer - cy mild, God and sin - ners rec - on - ciled."
Late in time be - hold Him come, Off - spring of a vir - gin's womb.
Light and life to all He brings, Ris'n with heal - ing in His wings.

Joy - ful, all you na - tions, rise; Join the tri - umph of the skies;
Veiled in flesh the God-head see! Hail, in - car - nate de - i - ty!
Mild He lays His glo - ry by, Born that we no more may die,

With an - gel - ic hosts pro - claim, "Christ is born in Beth - le - hem!"
Pleased as man with us to dwell, Je - sus, our Em - man - u - el!
Born to raise each child of earth, Born to give us sec - ond birth.

Refrain

Hark! The her - ald an - gels sing, "Glo - ry to the new - born king!"

Monday of the Second Week

Lighting

Light the Promise Candle and the Angel Candle. Ask the children to name each one.

Reading

Luke 1:26–38

Sing!

Take My Life, O Lord, Renew

Frances R. Havergal, 1836–79, alt.

PATMOS
William H. Havergal, 1793–1870

1 Take my life, O Lord, re-new, Con-se-crate my heart to You;
2 Take my hands and let them do Works that show my love for You;
3 Take my voice and let me sing Prais-es to my Sav-ior King;
4 Take my love; my Lord, I pour At Your feet its treas-ure store;

Take my mo-ments and my days; Let them sing Your cease-less praise.
Take my feet and lead their way, Nev-er let them go a-stray.
Take my lips and keep them true, Filled with mes-sag-es from You.
Take my self, Lord, let me be Yours a-lone e-ter-nal-ly.

Think about It

God had a very special purpose for a young girl named Mary. Because of that purpose, He spoke to her in a very special way—through the angel Gabriel. Mary believed the message, trusted in God, and obeyed Him with all of her heart. As a family, talk about Mary and her faith in God and His promise.

Who was Mary? She was a young girl who loved God and trusted in Him completely. Tradition suggests that she was probably 15 or so when the angel spoke to her.

Why did the angel Gabriel come to Mary? He came to deliver a message from God. It was wonderful news—God had chosen Mary to be the mother of His Son, Jesus.

Imagine for a minute that you are Mary. All of sudden an angel appears out of nowhere with this message: "You are going to have a baby. This baby will be special. He will be God's Son." Would you ask, "Who? Me?" Would you say, "I don't believe it?"

How did Mary react? She didn't do any of these things. She simply believed. She trusted God and said, "May it be to me as You have said" (Luke 1:38).

Does God have a plan for your life? God loved Mary and He loves you too. He had a plan for Mary and He has a plan for your life too. Just as Mary trusted God to work out His plan for her, you can trust Him to work out His plan for you.

Let's Pray

Dear God, help us to follow Mary's example and trust in You completely. Give us ears to hear You through Your words in the Bible. Fill each of us with the desire to follow You with all our heart. Through Jesus we pray. Amen.

Nativity Building

Place the angel and Mary figures close to one another. Then place one wrapped ornament per person next to the Advent wreath. Tell everyone that inside each package is an ornament, but that they will have to wait to see what their ornament looks like. Discuss how Mary must have felt—knowing that the baby Jesus was growing inside her, but having to wait to see what He looked like. (Note: You will open the ornaments later in the week.)

Tuesday of the Second Week

Lighting

Light the Promise and Angel Candles.

Reading

Matthew 1:18–25

Sing!

Oh, Come, Oh, Come, Emmanuel

Psalteriolum Cantionum Catholicarum, Köln, 1710
tr. John M. Neale, 1818–66, alt.

VENI EMMANUEL
French processional, 15th cent.

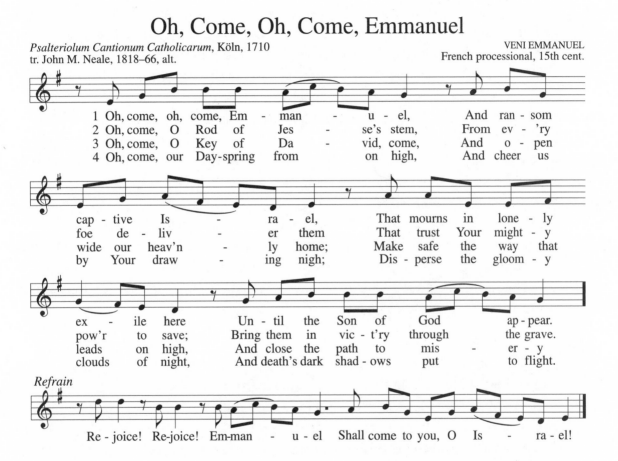

1 Oh, come, oh, come, Em - man - u - el, And ran - som
2 Oh, come, O Rod of Jes - se's stem, From ev - 'ry
3 Oh, come, O Key of Da - vid, come, And o - pen
4 Oh, come, our Day-spring from on high, And cheer us

cap - tive Is - ra - el, That mourns in lone - ly
foe de - liv - er them That trust Your might - y
wide our heav'n - ly home; Make safe the way that
by Your draw - ing nigh; Dis - perse the gloom - y

ex - ile here Un - til the Son of God ap - pear.
pow'r to save; Bring them in vic - t'ry through the grave.
leads on high, And close the path to mis - er - y
clouds of night, And death's dark shad - ows put to flight.

Refrain

Re - joice! Re-joice! Em-man - u - el Shall come to you, O Is - ra - el!

39

Think about It

Faith is believing in God and trusting His promises. Sometimes having faith requires doing something you may not want to do. It means believing in God and His Word even when things look impossible. That's what Joseph did after God's angel visited him in a dream.

What was Joseph's difficult decision? When Joseph found out that Mary was going to have a child, he didn't know if he should marry her or not. He didn't know what to do.

What was the angel's message? The angel told Joseph not to worry—Mary had not done anything wrong, and that he should not be afraid to take Mary as his wife.

What did the angel tell Joseph about the baby? The angel told Joseph that the baby Mary was going to have was God's Son—He would do great things. He should name the baby Jesus because He would save people from their sins. Joseph believed in God and trusted the message of the angel. He married Mary.

How does God speak to us today? God speaks to us through His Word and the special acts of Baptism and the Lord's Supper. He also speaks to us through His messengers of today who share God's Word (pastors, teachers, parents, other adults, and even kids). Through the work of the Holy Spirit, God reveals the good news of His love—that we have forgiveness and eternal life because of Jesus—and how to share His love with others.

Let's Pray

Dear God, help our faith to grow as we listen to Your Word and remember Jesus' love and forgiveness. Speak to us through pastors, teachers, and others as they share Your Word with us. Help us to trust in You and the promise of Your love. In Jesus' name. Amen.

Nativity Building

Place the angel and Joseph close to one another. Find creative ways to give messages of love to each other.

Wednesday of the Second Week

Lighting

Light the Promise and Angel Candles.

Reading

Matthew 2:13–15

Think about It

"Take the child and flee," God's angel told Joseph. Jesus' life was in danger. Herod had learned that a new king had been born and he was worried that this new king would take his place, so he ordered that all boys younger than two be killed. Jesus' life depended upon Joseph's obedience.

Why did Herod think that Jesus would take his place? Herod thought of Jesus as an earthly king, not as an eternal king. Herod did not understand that the kingdom of Jesus would be bigger, much bigger than his own small throne.

What is the difference between an earthly king and Jesus as heavenly king? The rule of an earthly king always comes to an end, but the kingship of Jesus will last forever. He has set us free from sin and He wants everyone to live forever in His kingdom.

Did Joseph question the angel's message or try to figure out his own solution? No. Joseph took Mary and Jesus and headed for Egypt immediately. It was the middle of the night, but Joseph didn't wait. He believed God's message and did what he was supposed to do.

Do we need to stop and wonder about God's promises to us? No. God loves us more than anything. He loves us so much that He sent Jesus, His only Son, to be our Savior. God watches over us and guides us. He even sends His angels to protect us. We never have to stop and question God and His love for us.

How can you know when God is speaking to you? God speaks to us through Word and

Sacrament. He made us His child through Baptism, and we can trust that He will equip us for every good work (2 Timothy 3:16–17). He will help us in all situations.

Sing!

Oh, Come, All Ye Faithful

John F. Wade, c. 1711–86; tr. composite

ADESTE FIDELES
John F. Wade, c. 1711–86

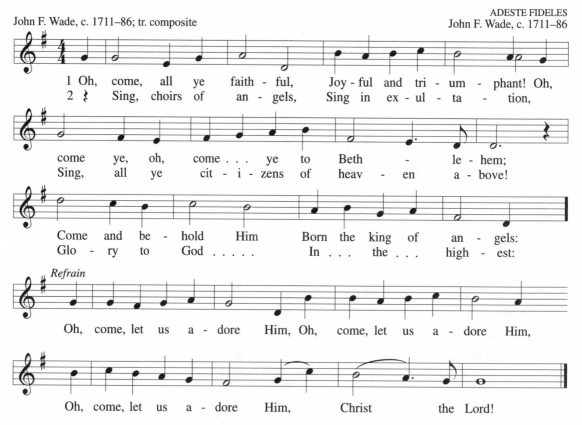

1 Oh, come, all ye faith - ful, Joy - ful and tri - um - phant! Oh,
2 Sing, choirs of an - gels, Sing in ex - ul - ta - tion,

come ye, oh, come . . . ye to Beth - le - hem;
Sing, all ye cit - i - zens of heav - en a - bove!

Come and be - hold Him Born the king of an - gels:
Glo - ry to God . . . . . In . . . the . . . high - est:

Refrain

Oh, come, let us a - dore Him, Oh, come, let us a - dore Him,

Oh, come, let us a - dore Him, Christ the Lord!

Let's Pray

Dear God, we pray for Your wisdom as we make decisions in life. Give us the courage to seek out Your will. Help us to trust that You only want what's best for us. Send Your Holy Spirit to help us obey You in all circumstances as quickly as Joseph. For Jesus' sake. Amen.

Nativity Building

Place the angel with Joseph and Mary. God never left Mary and Joseph alone. He was always there watching over them and sending His angel to guide and protect them. Talk about situations when you have obeyed without asking questions, just like Joseph.

Thursday of the Second Week

Lighting

Light the Promise and Angel Candles.

Reading

Matthew 7:7–8 and John 5:24

Think about It

Put on your listening ears. God is talking to us. Just as He spoke to Mary, Joseph, and the shepherds so long ago, God is talking to us as well. He speaks to us through His Word and as the Holy Spirit works through our pastors, teachers, parents, and even our friends to speak the word of God to us.

What happens when we listen to God? We learn about the many promises He makes to us and how He keeps them. We learn He is working out His plan for our lives. We learn about the many wonderful things God has done for us—especially how He showers us with His loving grace.

What are some of the wonderful things God has done for us? He made us, He sent Jesus to be our Savior from sin, and claimed us as His own through Baptism. He strengthens our faith through the power of the Holy Spirit and gives us special gifts to use for Him. The apostle James said, "Every good and perfect gift is from above, coming down from the Father" (James 1:17).

What do we have to do to receive God's gifts? We do not have to do anything to earn or to receive these gifts. God gives them to us because He loves us. We are His dear children because of the saving work of Jesus.

What are some specific gifts God has given your family this Christmas season?

Let's Pray

Dear Jesus, You know us by name and You are our Savior and very best Friend. Thank You for the many ways You speak to us. Forgive us for the times we don't hear Your voice or the times when we don't listen. Send Your Holy Spirit to open our ears and help us to pay attention to Your messages of love for us. Amen.

Sing!

God Is So Good

Anonymous   Anonymous

1 God is so good, God is so good,
2 I praise His name, I praise His name,
3 He an - swers prayer, He an - swers prayer,

God is so good, He's so good to me.
I praise His name, He's so good to me.
He an - swers prayer, He's so good to me.

Nativity Building

Hang an angel over the stable. Remind everyone that, as the time drew near, God put everything in place for the arrival of His Son on earth. He spoke to Joseph and Mary through the angels. He made sure there was a reason for Mary and Joseph to travel to Bethlehem. He made sure there was a place for Jesus to be born. All of this in order to keep His promise to send a Savior.

Friday of the Second Week

Lighting

Light the Promise and Angel Candles. Ask the children to name them as they are lit.

Reading

Luke 2:14–19

Think about It

Proclaim Jesus' birth with the angels. Worship at Jesus' feet with the shepherds. Think about the miracle of God's plan with Mary. The Messiah has been born. Rejoice! Send out the message: *Glory to God! We are freed from sin! Our Savior is born!*

When do we think about the good news of Jesus' birth? When do we share it with other people? Should it be only at Christmas or Easter? The news of God's love is too good to forget—we can rejoice in His love each and every day. We don't have to save it only for special occasions. God's love is not like Grandma's china—something to handle carefully, then store away until the next celebration. We can shout the news about Jesus, hear about His love for us, and live out our faith in Him every day.

Would you hide a favorite book under the bed? Would you set aside a favorite toy and never play with it? Would you keep from showing a favorite picture to friends? We wouldn't even think of hiding something we love from others. We want to share our special things with others. That's how it is with Jesus—we don't want to hide Him or the good news that He is our Savior. He is the Light of our life, our very best friend. Shine the light of Jesus by sharing the good news of His love with them every day.

How are you sharing Jesus' light to the world this Christmas? Discuss ways that you and your family have been like an angel, proclaiming the message of the Good News in the past. Think of some new ways to share His message this Christmas.

Sing!

Angels from the Realms of Glory

James Montgomery, 1771–1854, sts. 1–3
Salisbury Hymn Book, 1857, st. 4; alt.

REGENT SQUARE
Henry T. Smart, 1813–79

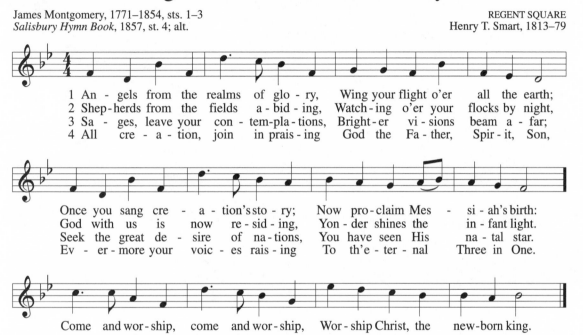

1 An - gels from the realms of glo - ry, Wing your flight o'er all the earth;
2 Shep-herds from the fields a - bid - ing, Watch-ing o'er your flocks by night,
3 Sa - ges, leave your con - tem-pla-tions, Bright-er vi - sions beam a - far;
4 All cre - a - tion, join in prais - ing God the Fa - ther, Spir - it, Son,

Once you sang cre - a - tion's sto - ry; Now pro-claim Mes - si - ah's birth:
God with us is now re - sid - ing, Yon - der shines the in - fant light.
Seek the great de - sire of na - tions, You have seen His na - tal star.
Ev - er - more your voic - es rais - ing To th'e - ter - nal Three in One.

Come and wor - ship, come and wor - ship, Wor - ship Christ, the new-born king.

Let's Pray

Dear Jesus, we want to proclaim Your name to everyone around us. We want to start here in our family and with our friends. Help us show Your love to each other, even when we don't feel like it. Use the Christmas cards we send to tell others about You as our Savior. Use the gifts we give to others to bring a smile and a message of love in and through You. Amen.

47

Nativity Building

Open the wrapped ornaments. As you do, talk about how you have waited and how you have looked forward to seeing what was inside. Think about the excitement Mary must have felt when she finally held baby Jesus for the first time. (Adults, tell the children how you felt as you waited for their arrival. Describe the first time you held them.)

Are You Ready for Jesus?

Therefore keep watch, because you do not know the day or the hour.

Matthew 25:13

Materials Needed This Week

Decorated Advent wreath with candles

Matches

A shiny coin for the nativity

Holy Bible

Some shepherds for the nativity

Star for the nativity

Townspeople for the nativity

Flashlight/pillow

Little mirror or magnifying glass for the nativity

Think about the life of Jesus and what He came to earth to accomplish. He gave up His glorious place in heaven and humbled Himself by coming into this world as a baby. The Bible says He made Himself to be nothing, and took on the role of servant. Even to the point of death—the humiliating death of the cross—Jesus remained focused on His purpose (Philippians 2:6-11). He did it for you. His love is that great.

Now it is our turn to respond to Jesus' love. Are you ready to give thanks for the wonderful gift of His great love for you? Are you ready to share that gift with your friends and family?

Let's Live It

As your family continues its preparations and celebrations, remember to ask "Are we ready for Jesus?"

1. Attend a Bethlehem fair or live nativity to experience what it might have been like in the town of Bethlehem the night Jesus was born.

2. Convey the spirit of Christmas by donating a gift to a homeless shelter, an organization for the needy, or a food pantry in your community.

3. While engaging in your holiday preparations—hanging stockings, wrapping gifts, baking goodies—talk about what it means to get ready for Christmas and receive Jesus' love.

4. Look at holiday celebrations in other cultures. How do they get ready? Compare the lavishness of our celebration with others, particularly those in third world nations. Is it still Christmas without all the frills?

5. Invite someone who would otherwise be alone to share Christmas with your family—perhaps foreign college students, single parents and their children, or senior citizens.

6.

7.

Saturday/Sunday of the Third Week

Lighting

Ask the children to name the first two candles. Does anyone know the name of this week's candle? It stands for rejoicing—rejoicing in our Savior's birth. It's the pink (or third blue) candle and it is called the Bethlehem Candle.

Reading

John 3:16–18 and James 1:17

Think about It

God was the greatest gift-giver in history—no one can give more than God. God knew we could not pay for our own sin, so He sent Jesus into the world to be our Savior. Because of Jesus, we receive God's gifts of grace—love, forgiveness, and eternal life.

Do special gifts have to cost a lot? Precious gifts may not always cost a lot of money, but they *do* cost the giver something. A special gift is given out of love for someone else.

What is a sacrificial gift? It is a gift offered at the giver's own expense. He or she takes something from themselves to give to someone they love. The sacrificial giver gives without expecting to receive anything in return.

Read the story of the widow who put two small coins into the offering box at the temple in Luke 21:1-4. Why did Jesus say that those coins were worth more than all of the money the rich man had given? It was because the widow's gift was a sacrifice. She had given all of her money—everything she had.

What did it cost God the Father to give us His gift? It cost Him the life of His only Son. Jesus gave up His place in heaven (Philippians 2:6-11) to come to earth and fulfill His Father's mission. In God's eyes you are worth the sacrifice—He loves you that much.

In the spirit of that kind of giving, what special gifts can you give? Whom do you want to thrill this Christmas? Remember that it doesn't take a lot of money; it takes a giving heart.

Sing!

Beautiful Savior

Gesangbuch, Münster, 1677
Tr. Joseph A. Seiss, 1823–1904

SCHÖNSTER HERR JESU
Silesian folk tune, 1842

1 Beau - ti - ful Sav - ior, King of cre - a - tion,
2 Fair are the mea - dows, Fair are the wood - lands,
3 Fair is the sun - shine, Fair is the moon - light,
4 Beau - ti - ful Sav - ior, Lord of the na - tions,

Son of God and Son of Man!
Robed in flow'rs of bloom - ing spring;
Bright the spar - kling stars on high;
Son of God and Son of Man!

Tru - ly I'd love Thee, Tru - ly I'd serve Thee,
Je - sus is fair - er, Je - sus is pur - er,
Je - sus shines bright - er, Je - sus shines pur - er
Glo - ry and hon - or, Praise, ad - o - ra - tion

Light of my soul, my joy, my crown.
He makes our sor - r'wing spir - it sing.
Than all the an - gels in the sky.
Now and for - ev - er - more be Thine!

54

Let's Pray

Dear God, You are awesome. Your gifts to us are amazing—far beyond our wildest dreams. As a family and as individuals, we say "yes" to your gift of Jesus. Whatever our situation, whatever our circumstances, help us to give our gifts in the same spirit through which You have given to us. In Jesus' name. Amen.

Nativity Building

Put a shiny coin in the stable as a reminder that special gifts don't cost a lot of money; they cost a part of our hearts.

Monday of the Third Week

Lighting

Light the first three candles. Now that three candles are lit, the light is shining brighter, clearer. Christmas is almost here.

Reading

Luke 2:1–7

Sing!

Away in a Manger

Unknown, c. 1883, sts. 1–2
John McFarland, 1851–1913, st. 3 alt.

AWAY IN A MANGER
American, 19th cent.

1 A - way in a man - ger, no crib for a bed, The lit - tle Lord
2 The cat - tle are low - ing, the ba - by a - wakes, But lit - tle Lord
3 Be near me, Lord Je - sus; I ask Thee to stay Close by me for -

Je - sus laid down His sweet head. The stars in the bright sky looked
Je - sus, no cry - ing He makes. I love Thee, Lord Je - sus. Look
ev - er, and love me, I pray. Bless all the dear chil - dren in

down where He lay, The lit - tle Lord Je - sus a - sleep on the hay.
down from the sky, And stay by my side un - til morn - ing is nigh.
Thy ten - der care, And take us to heav - en to live with Thee there.

Think about It

Mary and Joseph's trip to Bethlehem was dangerous, difficult, and exhausting. It took them many days to travel the 70 miles between Nazareth and Bethlehem. Yet, step by step, they were obedient to God and to the government that ordered the census.

What do you think Mary and Joseph's trip to Bethlehem was like? How was it different than the long trips our family takes? Mary and Joseph traveled most, if not all, of the way on foot. The roads were hot and dusty, and they carried everything they needed. They probably joined together with other small bands of travelers for safety and companionship.

What was God doing through Mary and Joseph's obedience? He was fulfilling His promise through them. Their journey was part of His plan formed long before as prophesied in Micah 5:2. The Savior would come from Bethlehem. The stage was being set. The main characters were moving into place. God's promise was coming true.

In what ways were Mary and Joseph obedient and how did God guide them? Mary and Joseph had eyes of faith, recognizing that God was directing their path, even to that small animal barn. God guided them one step at a time. They obeyed one step at a time.

Can we follow God today? God is calling for the same type of obedience in us today. He doesn't reveal our whole life's plan and say, "Now go out and do it, you're on your own." Instead, God gently leads us one step at a time.

Follow where God leads. Who knows what might happen!

Let's Pray

> Dear Lord, thank You for planning the path of our lives. Help us to follow You. Show us each step and light our direction so that there will be no doubt in us at all. In Your Word You have promised that Your yoke is easy and Your burden light (Matthew 11:30). Help us to trust in Your leading. Amen.

Nativity Building

Move Mary, Joseph, and the angel closer to the stable. Even though it was a long and difficult journey, Mary and Joseph were under God's care every step of the way.

Tuesday of the Third Week

Lighting

Light the first three candles. Can you name them in order?

Reading

Luke 2:1–8

Think about It

The streets were packed with jostling travelers, peddlers, and soldiers—all brought to Bethlehem because of the Roman census, a formal counting of the entire Roman empire. The people of the city were bustling here and there trying to take care of the needs of the growing crowd. Everyone was preoccupied.

Who were the people traveling to Bethlehem? How do you think they felt about being there? Many were people simply following government orders to return to the city of their birth; they might have been looking forward to meeting other family members from far away. Others were in Bethlehem selling goods and services to the travelers, excited at the thought of the money they would make. The soldiers were there to keep peace. Some of them might have been frustrated, on edge, or even bored with having to watch over the city and its people.

Do you think anyone noticed the young couple in obvious need? Did anyone stop to help them? Little did the people bumping into Joseph and Mary suspect the great event that was about to happen. Tradition suggests that Joseph was turned away several times by busy innkeepers before one of them noticed his wife's need. That innkeeper didn't offer much, but he offered what he had.

Could God have forced people to notice that He was coming into the world? Of course He could have, but God does not force Himself on anyone. He offers His love to everyone, but some refuse it. The innkeeper did not know it, but in his willingness to help the young couple, he provided a birthplace for the Kings of kings.

Does your life sometimes get so cluttered that you forget to look for God's presence? It is easy to let other things crowd God out of our lives. But the eyes of our faith are opened as we spend time in God's presence—listening to His Word and praying to Him each day.

Sing!

O Little Town of Bethlehem

Phillips Brooks, 1835–93

ST. LOUIS
Lewis H. Redner, 1831–1908

1 O little town of Beth-le-hem, How still we see thee
2 For Christ is born of Mar - y, And, gath-ered all a -
3 How si-lent-ly, how si-lent-ly The won-drous gift is
4 O ho-ly Child of Beth-le-hem, De-scend to us, we

lie! A-bove thy deep And dream-less sleep The si-lent stars go
bove While mor-tals sleep, The an-gels keep Their watch of won-d'ring
giv'n! So God im-parts To hu-man hearts The bless-ings of His
pray; Cast out our sin, And en-ter in, Be born in us to-

by; Yet in thy dark streets shin-eth The ev-er-last-ing
love. O morn-ing stars, to-geth-er Pro-claim the ho-ly
heav'n. No ear may hear His com-ing; But in this world of
day. We hear the Christ-mas an-gels The great glad tid-ings

light. The hopes and fears Of all the years Are met in thee to-night.
birth, And prais-es sing To God the king, And peace to all the earth!
sin, Where meek souls will Re-ceive Him, still The dear Christ en-ters in.
tell; Oh, come to us, A-bide with us, Our Lord Im-man-u-el.

Let's Pray

Dear Jesus, we give thanks that You do not judge us by what You see on the outside; You look inside our hearts and forgive us. We pray that the concerns and activities of this life never block our view of You and what You ask of us. Help us place You first amidst the activities of this holiday season. Amen.

Nativity Building

Add townspeople to the stable area. If your nativity set doesn't have townspeople, ask your children to select toys—action figures, small dolls, Lego creations, or others—that could be used to represent the people of Bethlehem.

Wednesday of the Third Week

Lighting

Light the first three candles. Name them as they are lit.

Reading

Psalm 46:10–11 and Revelation 3:20

Think about It

Everything is almost ready for the big day—the outside lights are up; the cards are in the mail; the tree is decorated, and packages are tumbling out from beneath it. Stores are packed with shoppers. Excited schoolchildren are restlessly squirming with impatience, eager for the final bell to ring.

> Your family has done a lot to prepare for Christmas. Take time to talk about some of the things you have done to get ready.

> *Are we as preoccupied as the people in Bethlehem?* It is easy to spend too much time focusing on ourselves—our gifts, our parties, and our programs. Christmas is Jesus' birthday. We are celebrating *Him* and the new life He gives to us. He wants us to take time to get to know Him better.

> *How have you been preoccupied this Christmas? How can you begin to put Jesus first?* Slow down a bit and spend time in God's Word. Let God remind You that His gifts of love, grace, and forgiveness are new each day. Then let Him help you share His love with other busy people around you.

Let's Pray

> Dear Jesus, we are sorry for the times we have not placed You first in our lives and in our Advent preparations. Thank You for Your patience, love, and forgiveness. Help us to remember that in all of our hustle and bustle You are with us every step of the way. Help us to take the time to share Your wonderful love with others. Amen.

Sing!

Take My Life, O Lord, Renew

Frances R. Havergal, 1836–79, alt.

PATMOS
William H. Havergal, 1793–1870

1 Take my life, O Lord, re - new, Con - se - crate my heart to You;
2 Take my hands and let them do Works that show my love for You;
3 Take my voice and let me sing Prais - es to my Sav - ior King;
4 Take my love; my Lord, I pour At Your feet its treas - ure store;

Take my mo - ments and my days; Let them sing Your cease - less praise.
Take my feet and lead their way, Nev - er let them go a - stray.
Take my lips and keep them true, Filled with mes - sag - es from You.
Take my self, Lord, let me be Yours a - lone e - ter - nal - ly.

Nativity Building

Move Mary and Joseph a little closer to the stable. They walked steadily each day to reach Bethlehem. Their journey is almost complete.

Thursday of the Third Week

Lighting

Light the first three candles. Name them in order. They are the Promise, Angel, and Bethlehem Candles.

Reading

Matthew 25:1–13

Think about It

Get ready? Get set? Wait.

Imagine you are getting ready for a race. You're at the starting line; your muscles are tense; your body is tight, ready to spring. You watch for the signal. Time seems to stand still. Until ... wait!

Who likes to wait? Who likes sitting in a crowded doctor's office? Or standing in slow-moving grocery store line? Or being on a long car ride? Or waiting as Mom talks on the phone? It's hard to wait.

Think of a time when you had to wait. Were you cranky and bored or did you pass the time wisely? How could you be more like the five wise young girls? The foolish girls wasted their time of waiting while the wise girls used their time to get ready for the bridegroom to arrive. That's what we can do—use the time of waiting to get our homes and our hearts ready. That's what the time of Advent is all about.

Does God ever wait? He waited for just the right time to send Jesus into this world. He's waiting now for just the right time to send Jesus back. He has already sent Jesus as Savior for everyone, and He waits for those who refuse His love to come to Him.

What other people in the Bible have waited? Abraham waited to become the father of a great nation. The children of Israel waited to be rescued out of slavery and to enter the Promised Land. Hannah waited for the Lord to give her a child, and David waited to be made king.

How did Mary wait? Mary waited nine months for Jesus' birth and then she waited another 30 years for His ministry to begin.

Today Christians look forward to Jesus' return. *How* we wait is almost as important as who we are waiting for. Are we cranky, bored, and unprepared for His coming? Or are we watchful and ready like the five wise girls in Jesus' parable? How are *you* waiting?

The Bible tells us to be ready for Jesus to come again. As we wait, we can joyfully share His love with others by shoveling a neighbor's sidewalk, helping Mom carry in the groceries, or playing a game with our little brother. We can stay tuned-in to God by going to church and Sunday school, listening to His word, and coming to Him in prayer. That's how we can keep the oil in our lamps burning.

Let's Pray

Dear Lord, help us to wait patiently—looking to You with eager-
ness in our hearts. Help us to live in Your forgiveness and be
ready for Your coming by loving You, following You, and sharing
the good news of Your love with others. Through You we pray.
Amen.

Nativity Building

Mary and Joseph have arrived at the stable. For the moment it is quiet. The animals are sleeping. Joseph is resting. Mary is laying some cloths in the manger. It is almost time for Jesus to be born.

Sing!

Give Me Oil in My Lamp

A. Sevison   Anonymous

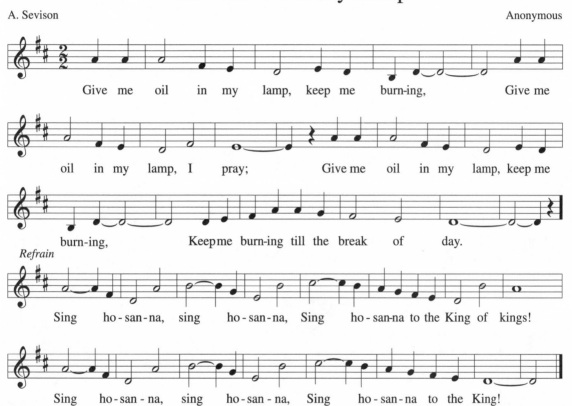

Give me oil in my lamp, keep me burn-ing, Give me
oil in my lamp, I pray; Give me oil in my lamp, keep me
burn-ing, Keep me burn-ing till the break of day.

Refrain

Sing ho-san-na, sing ho-san-na, Sing ho-san-na to the King of kings!

Sing ho-san-na, sing ho-san-na, Sing ho-san-na to the King!

Friday of the Third Week

Lighting

Light the first three candles. Name each candle as it is lit.

Sing!

This Little Gospel Light of Mine

Traditional   Traditional

1 This lit-tle Gos - pel light of mine, I'm going to let it shine;
2 All a - round the neigh-bor-hood I'm going to let it shine;
3 Hide it un - der a bush-el? No! I'm going to let it shine;

This lit-tle Gos - pel light of mine, I'm going to let it shine;
All a - round the neigh-bor-hood I'm going to let it shine;
Hide it un - der a bush-el? No! I'm going to let it shine;

This lit-tle Gos - pel light of mine, I'm going to let it shine,
All a - round the neigh-bor-hood I'm going to let it shine,
Hide it un - der a bush-el? No! I'm going to let it shine,

Let it shine all the time, Let it shine.
Let it shine all the time, Let it shine.
Let it shine all the time, Let it shine.

Reading

Matthew 5:14–16

Think about It

There are all kinds of light: starlight, candlelight, lamplight, headlights, and flashlights. Each kind of light casts its own special glow. Even Christmas lights flash and twinkle, brightening the area around them.

Jesus is the most important light. He is the source of all love and goodness. He will help us be lights to our families and communities, pointing the way to Jesus and His love.

What would happen if there was no light in this room? Would you be able to see very well? Take a flashlight and turn it on. Cover the flashlight with a pillow. Will the flashlight help you if its light is covered?

Jesus calls His believers the "light of the world." What is important about being the "light of the world"? As lights, we point others to God so they can all see Him and glorify Him (Matthew 5:14–16). God uses us to spread His love and goodness to others. Like the rays of light from a flashlight, we can be a source of God's light, pointing the way to Him.

How do you know that you are shining for Jesus? When you show love, kindness, thoughtfulness, and forgiveness because of what Jesus has done, you know that His love is shining through you. Let the rays of Jesus' light shine on everyone you meet. It is the greatest gift you can give.

What are some ways your light has shone to others this Christmas season? What ways can it still shine? Jesus said that whenever we treat someone with love and kindness—caring for their needs—it's the same as doing it to Him (Matthew 25:40). He also tells us to always treat others with love, the same way we would like to be treated (Matthew 7:12).

Let's Pray

Dear Jesus, give us Your love so that it might shine from us to others who may not yet know You. Help us to shine the light of Your love and forgiveness through our words and actions every day, and everywhere. In Your name we pray. Amen.

Nativity Building

Place a star above the nativity as if it is in the night sky, lighting the path of the Wise Men, and directing them from their homes far away to that little town in Judea.

Whom Did He Tell First?

*"I bring you good news
of great joy that will be for all the people."*

Luke 2:10b

Materials Needed This Week

Decorated wreath with candles

Matches

Holy Bible

Angels for the nativity

Shepherds for the nativity

Sheep for the nativity

Baby Jesus for the nativity

Baby picture of each family member

Candy canes hidden before Thursday's lesson

Paper with S-I-N written on it, one per person

Out of all the people in the world God could have told about Jesus' birth, He told the shepherds first. The town of Bethlehem was filled to overflowing with all kinds of people: peddlers, innkeepers, Roman soldiers, travelers, census takers. Yet, God chose lowly shepherds to be the first to hear His good news.

God sent angels to a group of shepherds on a lonely hillside to proclaim the message that would reverberate throughout the earth and across the spans of time: *The Savior is born!*

Let's Live It

As a family, celebrate that you have received the good news of Jesus' birth. You have heard the news and received Jesus' love.

1. Play "Name that Tune" with Christmas carols. Children who play instruments could be the song leaders, or if no instruments are available, family members can take turns humming the tune.

2. Have a birthday cake for Jesus with your dinner one night this week or on Christmas Eve.
3. As you give gifts to each other say, "Because God gave us the gift of Jesus, I give this gift to you with love."
4. Sing your children to sleep with carols.
5.

6.

Saturday/Sunday of the Fourth Week

Lighting

Ask the children to name each of the first three candles as they are lit. Light the fourth candle. It is the Shepherd Candle.

Reading

Luke 2:8–20

Think about It

God chose simple shepherds to be the first to hear the good news of Jesus' birth. Out on a lonely hillside they huddled together against the cold, watching the sheep while others slept.

Little did they know what glorious thing was about to happen. Little did they suspect that they would be the first to hear the most wonderful news ever told; a message that would travel around the world and across the spans of time: *The Savior is born!*

What made God choose shepherds out of all the people in Bethlehem? Maybe God knew how the shepherds would react to the message of the angels. They did not ask questions; they believed the report, worshiped and praised God, and shared the good news with others.

How did the shepherds respond to God's message? At first they were shocked and scared. But their fear quickly changed to excitement as they listened to the message delivered by the angels—the Savior had been born. Just as quickly, they acted on the message and went to Bethlehem to find the Savior. When they found Him, they worshiped Him.

Can you be like the shepherds, sharing the good news of Jesus' birth with others? Today's Bible reading tells that the shepherds shared what they had seen so freely that everyone who heard it wondered about it (Luke 2:18). Jesus wants you to share His love and forgiveness so freely that others will want to know more.

Has anyone ever told you something important? How did that make you feel? When friends tell us something special, they are trusting us with a precious treasure. Jesus is God's special treasure that He shared with us. We can worship Him from our hearts like the shepherds.

Let's Pray

Dear God, we glorify Your name and praise You. Help us to be more like the shepherds, immediately believing Your Word, worshiping You, and sharing Jesus' love with everyone we meet. In His name we pray. Amen.

Sing!

Hark! The Herald Angels Sing

Charles Wesley, 1707–88, alt.

MENDELSSOHN
Felix Mendelssohn, 1809–47

1 Hark! The her - ald an - gels sing, "Glo - ry to the new-born king;
2 Christ, by high - est heav'n a - dored, Christ, the ev - er - last - ing Lord,
3 Hail the heav'n-born Prince of Peace! Hail the sun of righ-teous-ness!

Peace on earth and mer - cy mild, God and sin - ners rec - on - ciled."
Late in time be - hold Him come, Off - spring of a vir - gin's womb.
Light and life to all He brings, Ris'n with heal - ing in His wings.

Joy - ful, all you na - tions, rise; Join the tri - umph of the skies;
Veiled in flesh the God-head see! Hail, in - car - nate de - i - ty!
Mild He lays His glo - ry by, Born that we no more may die,

With an - gel - ic hosts pro - claim, "Christ is born in Beth - le - hem!"
Pleased as man with us to dwell, Je - sus, our Em - man - u - el!
Born to raise each child of earth, Born to give us sec - ond birth.

Refrain

Hark! The her - ald an - gels sing, "Glo - ry to the new - born king!"

Nativity Building

Move the angels close to the shepherds. Divide your family into two groups. One group to roleplay the angels; the other to roleplay the shepherds. Have the angels sing praises to God as they share the good news. The shepherds show fear at first, then become joyful and praise God.

Monday of the Fourth Week

Lighting

Light all four candles. Have the children say the name of each as it is lit.

Reading

Luke 2:15–20

Think about It

After hearing the amazing message of the angels, the shepherds hurried into Bethlehem to see the newborn Savior, the Messiah that had been promised so long ago. Their excitement increased when they found Him lying in a manger.

The shepherds quickly told Mary and Joseph about the angels' visit and their search to find the baby. Not fully understanding what this baby would mean to all mankind, they knelt before Him and believed that God was doing something miraculous.

How can we have the excitement of the shepherds? We become more and more excited as the Holy Spirit works faith in our hearts. We can believe that God sent Jesus into this world to save us from our sins. We can believe that He has made us His own dear children. We can experience His love fresh each day. When we gather in God's name, the Bible says that He is among us. He lives in us today.

What was Mary's reaction to the shepherds' message? Mary had a quiet joy. She marveled at their words, remembering all that had happened. She knew God was doing something miraculous. Peace filled her heart as she recognized that they were truly in the presence of God.

Imagine that you are standing at the manger. How would you respond to everything that was happening? In our hearts, we *do* stand at the manger when we realize how much God has done for us through Jesus. Jesus gave up everything to come to earth and be our Savior. As we receive His forgiveness, mercy, and strength, we can experience the joy, love, and peace of Christmas all year long.

Jesus is called by many names in the Christmas story: Promised Messiah, Savior of the world, God's Son, Immanuel—God with us. Who do you say He is? The many names for Jesus all help us understand more deeply who He is. We know that Jesus is the Messiah God had promised long ago. By dying on the cross and paying the price for our sins, He became our Savior. God the Father calls Jesus His beloved Son. When He came to earth as a baby, everyone experienced the presence of God.

Let's Pray

Dear Jesus, be present in our hearts each day. Like the shepherds, we come to the manger to worship You as the promised Messiah, the Savior of the world. You are our Savior and Lord. Thank You for giving us Your life and Your love. Amen.

Sing!

Away in a Manger

Unknown, c. 1883, sts. 1–2
John McFarland, 1851–1913, st. 3 alt.

AWAY IN A MANGER
American, 19th cent.

1 A - way in a man - ger, no crib for a bed, The lit - tle Lord
2 The cat - tle are low - ing, the ba - by a - wakes, But lit - tle Lord
3 Be near me, Lord Je - sus; I ask Thee to stay Close by me for -

Je - sus laid down His sweet head. The stars in the bright sky looked
Je - sus, no cry - ing He makes. I love Thee, Lord Je - sus. Look
ev - er, and love me, I pray. Bless all the dear chil - dren in

down where He lay, The lit - tle Lord Je - sus a - sleep on the hay.
down from the sky, And stay by my side un - til morn - ing is nigh.
Thy ten - der care, And take us to heav - en to live with Thee there.

Nativity Building

Place the shepherds at the stable. Discuss how they stood in awe at the scene before them; a tiny baby lying in a manger who would change life on earth forever, the fulfillment of the promise of God.

Tuesday of the Fourth Week

Sing!

I Am Jesus' Little Lamb

Henrietta L. von Hayn, 1724–82; tr. composite

WEIL ICH JESU SCHÄFLEIN BIN
Brüder Choral-Buch, 1784

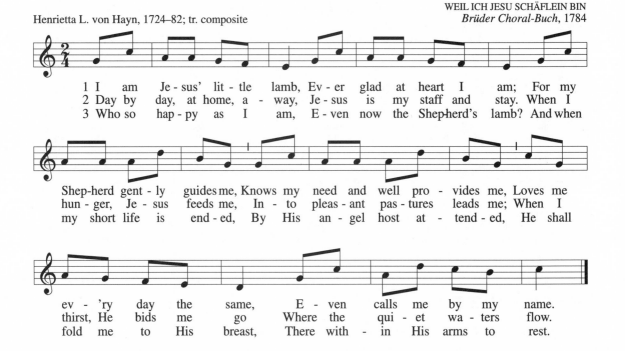

1 I am Je - sus' lit - tle lamb, Ev - er glad at heart I am; For my
2 Day by day, at home, a - way, Je - sus is my staff and stay. When I
3 Who so hap - py as I am, E - ven now the Shep-herd's lamb? And when

Shep-herd gent - ly guides me, Knows my need and well pro - vides me, Loves me
hun - ger, Je - sus feeds me, In - to pleas - ant pas - tures leads me; When I
my short life is end - ed, By His an - gel host at - tend - ed, He shall

ev - 'ry day the same, E - ven calls me by my name.
thirst, He bids me go Where the qui - et wa - ters flow.
fold me to His breast, There with - in His arms to rest.

Lighting

Light all four candles. Name each one and tell what they mean.

Reading

John 10:2–5, 11

Think about It

Sheep need a shepherd. Without one, they wander aimlessly through fields, falling into danger or scattering in fear. Sheep trust their shepherd completely. They listen for his voice and follow wherever he leads. Jesus told a parable about a shepherd with 100 sheep. He said that if one got lost, the shepherd would leave the 99 and search for the one that was lost (Luke 15:3–7). Every sheep is important to the shepherd. He loves and cares for each one.

How are we like sheep? We need to be taken care of—we need good food to eat, clothes to wear, and shelter to keep us warm and dry. We need someone to guide us and help us. We also need a Savior.

In what ways do sheep depend on the shepherd? How do we depend on Jesus? Sheep depend on the shepherd to provide for them and to keep them safe. We depend on Jesus in the same ways. He provides for our needs by placing us in the care of adults who love us. He guides us through His Word. And He gave His life to save us from sin.

Does Jesus even care about the small needs in our lives? Yes. Jesus wants to tenderly care for all of our needs. Even today, shepherds can be seen guiding their flocks and carrying young lambs or hurt sheep across their shoulders. Jesus is our Good Shepherd—watching over us, guiding us, and caring for our every need.

Would Jesus miss us if we stopped following Him? Jesus calls Himself the Good Shepherd. He gave His life so that we, His sheep, would not be lost forever in sin. He loves us and does not want anyone to be lost and to turn away from His love.

Let's Pray

Dear Jesus, thank You for providing all that we need: for loving us, for protecting us, for giving Your life for our sins, and for guiding us in all ways. Help us to trust You with even the small details of our lives, knowing that You are our Good Shepherd. Amen.

Nativity Building

Move all sheep to the manger. There is no better place to be than next to Jesus. He is our Good Shepherd. We want to stay close to Him—He loves us, leads us, and guides us.

Wednesday of the Fourth Week

Lighting

Have one child light all four candles. Ask the other children what each candle means as it is lit.

Reading

Jeremiah 31:3 and John 3:16–17

Think about It

The shepherds to whom the angels appeared did not hold important positions, were not well-known, and did not have a lot of money. They were, however, loved with an everlasting love. God reached out to each one with the most wondrous birth announcement: *Jesus is born!*

We may not hold important positions; we may not be sports stars or at the top of our class. But we, too, are loved with an everlasting love. That is reason to rejoice. This news is too good to keep to ourselves. God loves us! He has made a way for us to be His children. Jesus is that way.

What is an everlasting love? The word everlasting means to last throughout all time, or forever. An everlasting love means that there is no end to God's love for us. He loved us yesterday; He loves us today; He'll love us tomorrow. Nothing can separate us from God's love (Romans 8:38–39).

How do we know that God loves us with an everlasting love? The Bible tells us so. God's Word is truth and we can believe every word. In John 3:16 we read that God sent Jesus because He loved us. And because of Jesus, we will live eternally in heaven. That's all we need to know about God's everlasting love.

How about when we do something wrong—something called sin? Does God still love us then? Yes, He does! Nothing we do can make God stop loving us. God will not love *the sin*, but He will always love *us*. He has already forgiven our sins through Jesus. With the help of the Holy Spirit, we can turn away from sin and turn to Jesus instead.

Do you know someone this Christmas who needs to know God's everlasting love? Share Jesus today. Let His love fill you and overflow to those around you. He is a gift to be given over and over. Pray that God will direct you to tell a friend, a neighbor, or someone in your family about Jesus and His love.

Sing!

O Little Town of Bethlehem

ST. LOUIS

Phillips Brooks, 1835–93

Lewis H. Redner, 1831–1908

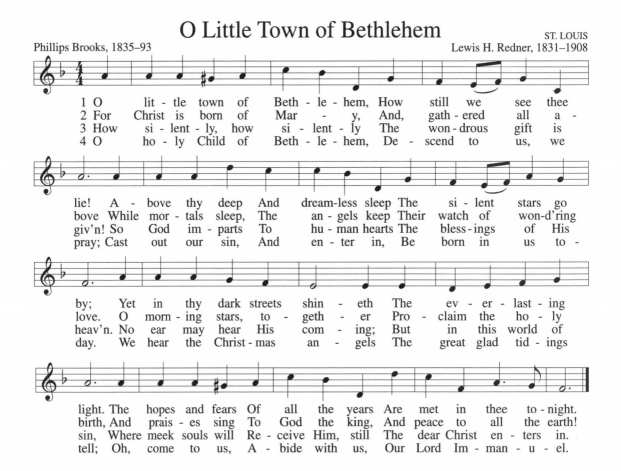

1 O lit - tle town of Beth - le - hem, How still we see thee
2 For Christ is born of Mar - y, And, gath - ered all a -
3 How si - lent - ly, how si - lent - ly The won - drous gift is
4 O ho - ly Child of Beth - le - hem, De - scend to us, we

lie! A - bove thy deep And dream-less sleep The si - lent stars go
bove While mor - tals sleep, The an - gels keep Their watch of won-d'ring
giv'n! So God im - parts To hu - man hearts The bless - ings of His
pray; Cast out our sin, And en - ter in, Be born in us to -

by; Yet in thy dark streets shin - eth The ev - er - last - ing
love. O morn - ing stars, to - geth - er Pro - claim the ho - ly
heav'n. No ear may hear His com - ing; But in this world of
day. We hear the Christ - mas an - gels The great glad tid - ings

light. The hopes and fears Of all the years Are met in thee to - night.
birth, And prais - es sing To God the king, And peace to all the earth!
sin, Where meek souls will Re - ceive Him, still The dear Christ en - ters in.
tell; Oh, come to us, A - bide with us, Our Lord Im - man - u - el.

Let's Pray

Dear God, we praise and thank You for Your everlasting love. We pray for our family and friends who still do not know that You sent Jesus as Savior. Help us to share Your saving love with them. In His name we pray. Amen.

Nativity Building

Arrange all of the figures around the manger. The time is drawing closer. Sing the songs of the angels—"glory to God in the highest." Rejoice with the shepherds—"we have found the Messiah." Quietly ponder all of these things in your heart with Mary. Jesus' coming is as fresh tonight as it was then.

Thursday of the Fourth Week

Lighting

Light all four candles. Name each one.

Reading

Isaiah 40:11

Think about It

(Before this devotion, quietly hide candy canes in easily accessible places.) As the devotion begins, direct the children to search for the candy canes hidden somewhere in the house.

A long time ago, a candy maker wanted to give the people in his town a Christmas gift that would remind them of God's love. He worked long and hard in his candy shop, fashioning a red-and-white peppermint stick into a shepherd's rod.

How does the hooked end of a shepherd's rod help the sheep? It is used to rescue the sheep when they are in danger—perhaps to pull them from a rocky ledge or out of a stream.

How can the straight end be of use? It is used as a weapon to protect the sheep, scaring away predators who would try to hurt the sheep.

Why would the candy maker use the color white? White reminds us that Jesus was pure and without sin. Even though He came to earth as a man, He was also true God and He had no sin.

Why would the candy maker use the color red? The color red reminds us that Jesus shed His blood for our sin. Jesus took our punishment. He paid the price for each and every sin.

In what other ways does the candy cane remind you of Jesus? The candy is hard. This reminds us that Jesus is the rock of our faith. If you hold the candy cane upside down, it will look like the letter 'J' which stands for Jesus, our Good Shepherd.

Just as you looked for the candy canes that were hidden, remember that the Good Shepherd searches for lost sheep, not stopping until they are all found. People who don't know about Jesus, or do not follow Him, are like the lost sheep.

Sing!

Amazing Grace

NEW BRITAIN

John Newton, 1725–1807, alt.

J. Carrell and D. Clayton, *Virginia Harmony*, 1831

1 A - maz - ing grace! How sweet the sound That
2 The Lord has prom - ised good to me, His
3 Through man - y dan - gers, toils, and snares I
4 Yes, when this flesh and heart shall fail And

saved a wretch like me! I once was lost but
word my hope se - cures; He will my shield and
have al - read - y come; His grace has brought me
mor - tal life shall cease, A - maz - ing grace shall

now am found, Was blind but now I see!
por - tion be As long as life en - dures.
safe so far, His grace will see me home.
then pre - vail In heav - en's joy and peace.

85

Let's Pray

Dear Jesus, You are our Good Shepherd. Thank You for all of the reminders of Your saving love, even the candy cane. Help us to share the truth of Your love with others so that the lost can be found and know Your saving love. Amen.

Nativity Building

Put a candy cane in the stable as a reminder that Jesus is our Good Shepherd.

Friday of the Fourth Week

Lighting

Light all four candles. Jesus is your light shining through the darkness of sin in this world.

Reading

Isaiah 53:6–7 and John 1:29

Think about It

Imagine that God is on one side of a huge canyon and you are stuck on the other side. A heavy fog makes it difficult to see Him clearly, but you know He's there. Then comes Jesus as the Son who burns away the fog of sin separating us from God the Father.

Jesus took the punishment for all the wrong things we have ever done. Jesus took our punishment so that we could be called the children of God. He erased our sin and set us free. He did all that it took to open the path back to God. We are children who can freely talk to God our Father, get to know Him, and have a relationship with Him.

How do we receive forgiveness? We receive forgiveness through Jesus' death and resurrection. He forgives all of our sins and draws us closer to God the Father. Just like the shepherds who first were afraid, our fears can be changed to rejoicing.

What does it mean that Jesus was punished for our sins? It is like your brother or sister saying to Mom or Dad, "I'll take Jimmy's time out. Punish me, don't punish him." Imagine that you broke a house rule, but your sister offered to take your punishment. That's what Jesus did. He took the punishment that we actually deserved.

Give each person a piece of paper with the word S-I-N written on it. Hold the paper directly in front of your face. Can you see anyone? Can anyone see you? Sin keeps us from seeing Jesus. Crumple up the paper. Now we can see. Jesus came to earth to take the punishment for our sins and set us free. The barrier of sin is gone. We can approach the heavenly Father in love and thanksgiving.

Let's Pray

Dear Jesus, help us to see the sin in our lives so that we can turn it over to You. Thank You for taking our punishment so we would not have to suffer the eternal punishment of hell. Help us to turn away from sin. May our words and actions bring glory to You. Amen.

Sing!

What Child Is This

William C. Dix, 1837–98

GREENSLEEVES
English ballad, 16th cent.

1 What child is this, who, laid to rest, On Mar-y's lap is sleep-ing?
2 Why lies He in such mean es-tate Where ox and ass are feed-ing?

Whom an-gels greet with an-thems sweet While shep-herds watch are keep-ing?
Good Chris-tian, fear; for sin-ners here The si-lent Word is plead-ing.

This, this is Christ the King, Whom shep-herds guard and an-gels sing;
Nails, spear shall pierce Him through, The cross be borne for me, for you;

Haste, haste to bring Him laud, The babe, the son of Mar-y!
Hail, hail the Word made flesh, The babe, the son of Mar-y!

Nativity Building

Put the crumpled papers at the stable. Jesus came to take away all our sins.

88

Congratulations!

Your Savior Is Born!

. . . you are to give Him the name Jesus,

because He will save His people from their sins.

Matthew 1:21.

Lighting

Light all four outer candles naming them as they are lit. Light the Christ Candle (white pillar candle in the middle) as the children shout, "Jesus is born!" Tonight this candle stands for Jesus' first coming into this world. It is white to symbolize His holiness and purity.

Sing!

Silent Night, Holy Night

Joseph Mohr, 1792–1848
Tr. John F. Young, 1820–85

STILLE NACHT
Franz Gruber, 1787–1863

1 Si - lent night, ho - ly night! All is calm, all is bright
2 Si - lent night, ho - ly night! Shep - herds quake at the sight;
3 Si - lent night, ho - ly night! Son of God, love's pure light

Round yon vir - gin moth-er and child. Ho - ly In - fant, so ten - der and mild,
Glo - ries stream from heav-en a - far, Heav'n - ly hosts .. sing, Al - le - lu - ia!
Ra - diant beams from Your ho - ly face With the dawn of re - deem - ing grace,

Sleep in heav - en - ly peace, Sleep in heav - en - ly peace.
Christ, the Sav - ior, is born! Christ, the Sav - ior, is born!
Je - sus, Lord, at Your birth, Je - sus, Lord, at Your birth.

Reading

Luke 1:31

Think about It

The day we were promised—the day we have been preparing for and have been expecting—is finally here. We rejoice as we remember how our Savior entered the world as a tiny, innocent baby. It is an event that changed the course of history forever. God set in motion His plan to free humanity from slavery to sin. He came to do it Himself.

What is God's gift to us this Christmas season? It is Himself. He was called Immanuel which means God with us. Through Jesus God extends His love and forgiveness to you. Receive it with excitement.

Rejoice that your Savior has come! Worship Him by singing as many songs as your family desires.

Let's Pray

Dear Jesus, thank You for being my own personal gift from God. You bring healing for all my hurts and disappointments. You bring forgiveness for all my sins. Help me to follow the example of Your godly life. Thank You for loving me. In Your name. Amen.

Nativity Building

Place the baby Jesus into the manger as you sing "Away in a Manger." Throw away the pieces of crumpled paper. Jesus removes our sin. It is no more.

"I Will Come Again"

In the last days the mountain of the Lord's temple

will be established as chief among the mountains . . .

and all nations will stream to it.

Isaiah 2:2

Lighting

Light all five candles today. Today the Christ Candle stands for Jesus' second coming, the promise we still anticipate. (Place baby pictures of each family member around the wreath.)

Sing!

Joy to the World

Isaac Watts, 1674–1748, alt.

ANTIOCH
George F. Handel, 1685–1759, adapt.

1 Joy to the world, the Lord is come! Let earth re - ceive its
2 Joy to the earth, the Sav - ior reigns! Let all their songs em -
3 No more let sin and sor - row grow Nor thorns in - fest the
4 He rules the world with truth and grace And makes the na - tions

King; Let ev - 'ry heart pre - pare Him
ploy While fields and floods, rocks, hills, and
ground; He comes to make His bless - ings
prove The glo - ries of His righ - teous -

room And heav'n and na - ture sing, And heav'n and na - ture
plains Re - peat the sound - ing joy, Re - peat the sound - ing
flow Far as the curse is found, Far as the curse is
ness And won - ders of His love, And won - ders of His

sing, And heav'n, and heav'n and na - ture sing.
joy, Re - peat, re - peat the sound - ing joy.
found, Far as, far as the curse is found.
love, And won - ders, won - ders of His love.

94

Reading

Isaiah 9:6–7 and Revelation 21:3–4

Think about It

Look at the babies in the pictures. *Who are these babies in the pictures?* Just as we grew, Jesus grew too. He lived life here on earth and now He is King in heaven and in our hearts.

What do today's passages say about Jesus' kingdom? Long before Jesus' birth, God told the prophet Isaiah that Jesus' kingdom would have no end. It would be built on justice and righteousness.

It would be built within our hearts as we believe in Him as our Savior from sin (John 3:1–3); and on a day yet to come, Jesus will return. He will wipe away all tears, pain, and sin (Revelation 21:3–4). Every knee shall bow and every tongue will confess that He is Lord.

What can we do while we wait? Remember that Jesus is our King right now. He is King in heaven and He is King in our lives. Start each day confessing that He is your Lord. Love and serve Him with all your whole heart and with all your soul and with all your strength (Deuteronomy 6:5). Wait hopefully, knowing that God keeps His promises.

Let's Pray

Dear Jesus, thank You for reigning in our hearts, and for loving, guiding, directing, and forgiving us. Continue to teach us Your ways and guide us so we can walk in Your path. You are the Wonderful Counselor, the Mighty God, the Everlasting Father, and the Prince of Peace. Amen.

Nativity Building

There is nothing to add today. Move the figures and retell the story of Jesus' birth.

Seek and You Will Find

Jesus said, "I praise You, Father, Lord of heaven and earth,

because You have hidden these things from the wise and learned,

and revealed them to little children."

Matthew 11:25

Materials Needed This Week

Christ Candle from Advent wreath

Matches

Holy Bible

Wise Men for the nativity

Small candle

Small cross

Gold coin, incense, herb

Small wrapped package

Family picture

Magnifying glass

A bright fire in your fireplace (if you have one)

A pearl or marble for each child to be hidden before Day Two

Things of value are looked for, sought after, or worked for. Jesus said, "Ask and it will be given to you; seek and you will find; knock and the door will be opened to you" (Matthew 7:7).

Would the shepherds have received the blessing of seeing the Messiah if they had not acted on what the angels told them? Would the Wise Men have found the infant king if they had not followed the star? The shepherds and the Wise Men responded through faith and trust. They did not even know the ending to Jesus' story. We do! How can we respond to His love for us?

Let's Live It

Even though Christmas day has come and gone, remember that we can seek Jesus each day of the year.

1. As you begin to take down your Christmas decorations, focus your attention on the nativity. Its message lasts all year.

2. Have a special family night on January 6 to celebrate Epiphany. Invite another family to join your celebration.

3. Let your children roleplay the Christmas story several ways—using the nativity figurines, using their toys as different characters, or putting on a play.

4. Spend a special afternoon or evening together burning your own Yule log. Get each family member involved in making a snack, picking out a game, or reading a book together.

5.

6.

Day One of Epiphany

Lighting

Light the Christ Candle. Jesus is our light. He guides His followers by His light.

Reading

Matthew 5:14–16 and John 8:12

Think about It

Many years ago in merry old England, the people had a custom of burning a huge log in their fireplaces beginning on Christmas Eve. The Christmas festivities would continue for as many days as the Yule log burned. These days came to be called the "twelve days of Christmas."

At first the log burned hot—bright, bold, and exciting. Then the celebration was in full swing—much like our homes on Christmas Eve and Christmas morning. But slowly the flames died until only a few flickers remained. By now your Christmas celebrations have settled down, becoming like glowing embers.

Share the special memories of this Christmas season with each other. What was your favorite part? Was it opening presents? Was it going to church? Or was it going to Grandma's house and visiting with your family? Sharing the memories brings them alive all over again.

How did Jesus bless you this Christmas? Did you learn more about Him than you knew before? How did He touch your life and that of your family? Jesus is so wonderful to us. He forgives our sins and gives His love to us without asking for anything in return. You can respond to His love through sharing His love with others.

How can your family keep the Christmas spirit alive all year? What kinds of things can you do to share the love of Jesus with others? Perhaps your family could volunteer at a homeless shelter, or donate needed items to one. Maybe you can adopt a grandma or grandpa in your neighborhood who would enjoy doing things with your family. Perhaps you can talk to your pastor and find out how to support a missionary family. Whatever you decide, let the spirit of Jesus' light burn in your hearts all year. The glow of Christmas will go on and on and on.

Let's Pray

Dear God, even though the packages are gone from under the tree
and the decorations are being put away, we thank You for Your
love that never changes. Help us to continue to seek ways to live
in Your light and shine the message of Your love and forgiveness
to others. In Jesus' name. Amen.

Sing!

This Little Gospel Light of Mine

Traditional   Traditional

1 This lit-tle Gos - pel light of mine, I'm going to let it shine;
2 All a - round the neigh-bor-hood I'm going to let it shine;
3 Hide it under a bush-el? No! I'm going to let it shine;

This lit-tle Gos - pel light of mine, I'm going to let it shine;
All a - round the neigh-bor-hood I'm going to let it shine;
Hide it under a bush-el? No! I'm going to let it shine;

This lit-tle Gos - pel light of mine, I'm going to let it shine,
All a - round the neigh-bor-hood I'm going to let it shine,
Hide it under a bush-el? No! I'm going to let it shine,

Let it shine all the time, Let it shine.
Let it shine all the time, Let it shine.
Let it shine all the time, Let it shine.

Nativity Building

Put a small, unlit candle near the stable to remind you that Jesus is the source of our light. He is the reason for our joy.

Day Two of Epiphany

Lighting

Light the Christ Candle. Jesus is our Treasure.

Reading

Matthew 13:44–46

Think about It

(Before this devotion, quietly hide the pearl or marble in easily accessible place.) Search for the pearl (or marble) that has been hidden somewhere in the room. Things we really like are valuable to us. We take special care of them and handle them gently. They are like beautiful, glittering pearls that are beautiful to look it and to hold. Jesus' love and God's truth are like the most precious of gems.

The men in these parables wanted their treasures more than anything else in their lives. They sold everything they had in order to buy them. *Is there anything in your life for which you would sell everything else?* It would have to be something very special indeed to sell everything you had in order to get it.

Have you ever wanted something really, really badly—so badly that it was all you could think about? What happened when you got it? When we first get something we've really wanted, we are excited. We play with it or use it all the time. But after awhile we might get tired of it, or want something else. Material things in the world are fun to have, but they are not real treasures.

What was the real treasure Jesus was teaching about in the parable? The real treasure is the kingdom of heaven—it is worth giving up everything else. The kingdom of heaven is found in Jesus. It is the treasure we have through believing in Him.

What does Jesus say in Matthew 6:21? Wherever our treasure is, our heart will be also. Whatever we prize most—something we own, a friendship we have with someone, a desire we have, or maybe even something we received for Christmas—will receive our time and devotion.

Where is your treasure today? God wants us to love Jesus more than anything else. He doesn't order us to give up everything else, but He desires that we will not let anything else be more important than our love for Him.

Sing!

Jesus Loves Me, This I Know

Anna B. Warner, 1820–1915   William B. Bradbury, 1816–68

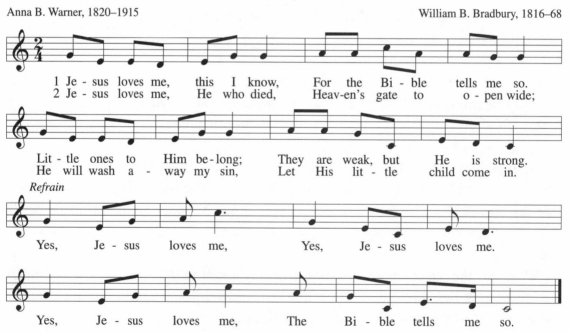

1 Je - sus loves me, this I know, For the Bi - ble tells me so.
2 Je - sus loves me, He who died, Heav-en's gate to o - pen wide;

Lit - tle ones to Him be - long; They are weak, but He is strong.
He will wash a - way my sin, Let His lit - tle child come in.

Refrain

Yes, Je - sus loves me, Yes, Je - sus loves me.

Yes, Je - sus loves me, The Bi - ble tells me so.

102

Let's Pray

Dear God, help us to follow You with our whole hearts. We thank You for all the material blessings You have given us, and for all the desires, dreams, and goals You have placed in our lives. We confess that sometimes we make these things more important than You. Help us keep each one in its rightful place behind You and Your lordship in our lives. In Jesus' name. Amen.

Nativity Building

Place the pearl (or marble) close to the manger. The treasures of earth are beautiful, but no treasure is greater than Jesus.

Day Three of Epiphany

Lighting

Light the Christ Candle. Jesus is our Glory.

Reading

Acts 6:5–7:1, 54–60

Sing!

Let Us Ever Walk with Jesus

Sigismund von Birken, 1626–81
Tr. *Lutheran Book of Worship*, 1978, alt.

LASSET UNS MIT JESU ZIEHEN
Georg G. Boltze, 1788

1 Let us ev - er walk with Je - sus, Fol - low His ex - am - ple pure,
2 Let us suf - fer here with Je - sus And with pa - tience bear our cross.

Through a world that would de - ceive us And to sin our spir - its lure.
Joy will fol - low all our sad - ness; Where He is, there is no loss.

On - ward in His foot - steps tread - ing, Pil - grims here, our home a - bove,
Though to - day we sow no laugh - ter, We shall reap ce - les - tial joy;

Full of faith and hope and love, Let us do our Fa - ther's bid - ding,
All dis - com - forts that an - noy Shall give way to mirth here - af - ter.

Faith - ful Lord, with me a - bide; I shall fol - low where You guide.
Je - sus, here I share Your woe; Help me there Your joy to know.

Think about It

Following Jesus calls for sacrifice—giving up or putting aside something you really want. Sometimes the cost of following Jesus means not doing something you think you would really like to do, such as watching certain movies or listening to certain kinds of music that do not glorify God.

Sometimes following Jesus means obeying your parents when you would rather not. Or being truthful when it seems easier to lie. Or choosing to forgive someone who hurt you. In certain parts of the world, following Jesus can even cost you your life. Christians are still dying or being hurt because of their faith in Jesus.

Stephen died because of his faith. What did he do that caused his death? Stephen died because he professed that he believed in Jesus. Stephen was a leader in his church. He taught others about Jesus. The Jewish leaders were afraid of the things Stephen said and did. They did not want people following Jesus.

What did some of the members of the Synagogue do? (A Synagogue is a Jewish church). They told lies about Stephen and turned the people who had been listening to him against him. Then they took Stephen to the Jewish leaders.

Did the Jewish leaders listen to Stephen? How did they react? The leaders were so upset by Stephen's words that they had him stoned to death. They closed their hearts and minds to God. Yet even at his death, Stephen did not waver in his love for Jesus. He prayed for God to forgive the people who were killing him. He was faithful to the end.

Have you ever sacrificed something because you stood up for Jesus? Or even because you were known as His follower? We may not be stoned to death for our faith, but we might suffer in other ways. Adults, share a time when you had to choose to stand up for your faith.

Let's Pray

> Dear Lord, help us learn from Stephen's example of faithfulness. We pray that You would help us take a strong stand for You in our everyday lives at home, at work, and at school. We pray for our Christian brothers and sisters around the world who are faced with the same life-and-death choice as Stephen. Give them the faith to stand strong. In Your name. Amen.

Nativity Building

Place a small cross in the stable. Remember that Jesus sacrificed His life for us and that following Jesus involves our own sacrifices.

Day Four of Epiphany

Lighting

Light the Christ Candle. Jesus is the Great Giver.

Sing!

Sing "We Three Kings" as found on page 108.

Reading

Matthew 2:9–12

Think about It

The Wise Men, or Magi, were first in a long line of gift givers. Today's passage records the first gift exchange of Christmas. God the Father gave the gift of His Son, and the Wise Men gave the gift of their treasures. These gifts were wrapped in love.

God could give no greater gift to His creation than His beloved Son Jesus, who in turn would give us the gift of eternal life. The Wise Men could give no greater gifts than their precious treasures of gold, incense, and myrrh.

How are each of these gifts the same? Each giver gave their very best. God gave us His

106

best in Jesus. Jesus gives us His best in the gift of eternal life. The Wise Men gave the best from their earthly wealth. The spirit of this kind of giving happens when we receive the special gift of Jesus and give our love and devotion to Him in return.

How did the Wise Men offer their gifts to Jesus? What do you think they were thinking and feeling? They offered their gifts to the new King in respect and reverence. The Bible says they fell down and worshiped Jesus. These important earthly men, who probably did not bow to very many people, bowed to Jesus, their heavenly King.

The Wise Men gave gifts of gold, frankincense, and myrrh. What extra meaning did these gifts have? Gold is the most precious of metals; only powerful kings had great storehouses of gold. Frankincense comes from tree sap and when burned it gives off a lovely, spicy fragrance; it was burned as part of worship. Myrrh is a fragrance too; it was made into an ointment used during burials. Through these gifts, the Wise Men declared that Jesus was King, God, and Savior.

Let's Pray

Dear Jesus, thank You that even these gifts given so long ago can remind us today of who You really are. We recognize You as our King. We want to live our lives according to Your will. We recognize You as our God. You sit on a heavenly throne and have authority over everything. We recognize You as our Savior. Forgive us for each wrong word, thought, and action. In Your name we pray. Amen.

Nativity Building

Place your own "Wise Men" gifts at the stable—a coin reminding us that the kingdom of Jesus is most precious, incense reminding us that Jesus is the God we worship, and a bitter herb reminding us that He suffered for our salvation.

Day Five of Epiphany

Lighting

Light the Christ Candle. Jesus received meaningful gifts.

Sing!

We Three Kings of Orient Are

John H. Hopkins, Jr., 1857

KINGS OF ORIENT
John H. Hopkins, Jr., 1857

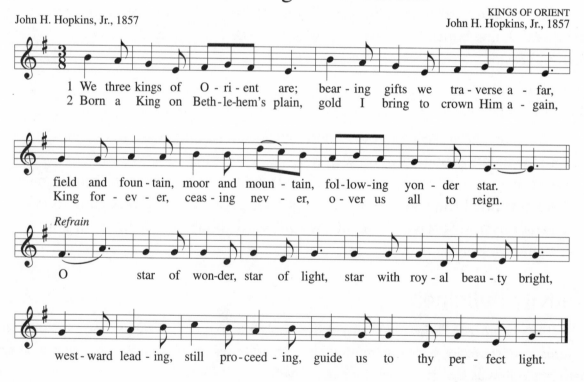

1 We three kings of O - ri - ent are; bear - ing gifts we tra - verse a - far,
2 Born a King on Beth - le - hem's plain, gold I bring to crown Him a - gain,

field and foun - tain, moor and moun - tain, fol - low - ing yon - der star.
King for - ev - er, ceas - ing nev - er, o - ver us all to reign.

Refrain

O star of won - der, star of light, star with roy - al beau - ty bright,

west - ward lead - ing, still pro - ceed - ing, guide us to thy per - fect light.

Reading

Matthew 2:11; Luke 6:38; and 2 Corinthians 9:7–8

Think about It

Just think—special gifts given to Jesus by those who followed the light of a star to find Him. These three special gifts still remind us of who Jesus is and what place He holds in our lives as King, God, and Savior. The Wise Men gave these gifts from their hearts. We can too.

The special gifts that we give to God and others come from the heart. They show our love and our care. They need not cost a lot to bring joy to the receiver.

Was there someone for whom you searched for the perfect gift this Christmas season? You probably thought hard about what that person would like. Perhaps you looked at many things before finding the special gift that would show your love. When the gift was opened, you waited for that burst of surprise that told you that person was pleased. *Your* joy was in the giving. *Their* joy was in knowing your love.

How have you and your family given "cheerfully" this Christmas season? In Matthew 25:40 Jesus tells us that whenever we give food to the hungry, a drink to the thirsty, or clothing to the poor, we have done it for Him. In other words, we serve Jesus every time we meet a need and serve someone else.

Read today's Bible passages again. *If we give all of our gifts out of love, will we ever run out of gifts to give?* In Luke Jesus says that if we give fully the same will be given back to us and more. In 2 Corinthians we learn that God gives abundantly for every good deed. We will never run out of love when it is God's love we are sharing. Love is from God and it flows from Him freely. Never be afraid to give all you have. God will fill you to overflowing with His love.

What kind of gift can we give to Jesus? We can give Him our hearts. We can love and serve Him by loving and serving others. He will grant us His love, peace, and joy as we live to serve Him.

Let's Pray

Dear God, thank You for Your wonderful love. Help us to give of ourselves and to show Your love through everything we say and do. Help us to look for ways to serve You through things that help others today. In Jesus' name. Amen.

Nativity Building

Place a small wrapped package at the stable. Remember that we give the gifts of our love to Jesus through obedience and service.

Day Six of Epiphany

Lighting

Light the Christ Candle. Jesus finds joy in us.

Reading

John 15:12–17 and Romans 12:1–2

Think about It

God our Creator reached out in love that first Christmas when He sent Jesus to us. He wanted to rescue us from our sin, to bring us out of darkness. He wanted us to know how very much He loves us.

What He got in return were a variety of responses. The shepherds and Wise Men worshiped Him. The people in Bethlehem ignored Him. King Herod hated Him. What will our response be today?

Visit the manger in your heart. What gift will you bring to Jesus? Give Him yourself. Jesus wants every one of us: moms, dads, boys, and girls. He wants our love and obedience. He wants us to trust Him completely. He gives us forgiveness, grace, and everlasting life.

What makes the giving of ourselves such a special gift to Jesus? God didn't make us to be robots who have no choice in what we do. No indeed! In bringing us to faith in Jesus, He gives us freedom to choose how we live our lives; freedom to love and follow Him in response to His love for us. When our actions, our thoughts, and our attitudes show that we love Jesus and accept what He has done for us, we are giving Jesus the greatest gift we can give.

According to today's Bible passages, how can we bring Jesus joy? Jesus gave the gift of Himself when He died on the cross for our sins. When Jesus sees us giving of ourselves out of love for others, He takes joy in us. Imagine that! We bring joy to Jesus by following the example of His love.

Jesus loved us enough to give us the very best; can we give Him anything less in return? Start giving the gift of yourself today.

Let's Pray

Dear Jesus, give us grateful hearts that will give to others in love. Fill us
with the power of Your Holy Spirit so that we might walk in Your ways
and follow Your command to love others. We love You, Jesus. Amen.

Nativity Building

Place a family picture by the stable. We can give ourselves as a gift to Jesus. We don't have to wait until we change, or grow, or become better in some way. Jesus loves us just way we are. He takes joy in us just the way we are.

Sing!

What Child Is This

William C. Dix, 1837–98

GREENSLEEVES
English ballad, 16th cent.

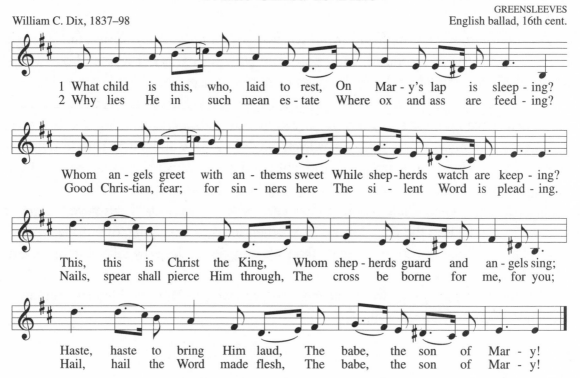

1 What child is this, who, laid to rest, On Mar-y's lap is sleep-ing?
2 Why lies He in such mean es-tate Where ox and ass are feed-ing?

Whom an-gels greet with an-thems sweet While shep-herds watch are keep-ing?
Good Chris-tian, fear; for sin-ners here The si-lent Word is plead-ing.

This, this is Christ the King, Whom shep-herds guard and an-gels sing;
Nails, spear shall pierce Him through, The cross be borne for me, for you;

Haste, haste to bring Him laud, The babe, the son of Mar-y!
Hail, hail the Word made flesh, The babe, the son of Mar-y!

Day Seven of Epiphany

Lighting

Light the Christ Candle. Jesus draws all people to Himself.

Reading

Matthew 2:1–10

Think about It

As God joyfully announced the birth of Jesus to shepherds on a lonely hillside in Bethlehem, He quietly set His star in the night sky and waited.

Soon the band of Wise Men saw His sign and began seeking Him. They left their homes, families, and country in search of the meaning of that star. It was a search that took a long time to complete.

Who were these Wise Men and what made them follow a star? Maybe they were astrologers or observers of stars from the Far East. Maybe they were really kings. The Bible states that they were Magi. Throughout history, they have been called Wise Men.

They saw the new star and studied. They learned that God said He would set a new star in the sky to announce the birth of a new king. They came to Herod and said, "We have seen His star in the east and have come to worship Him." They recognized that something miraculous was happening in the heavens and they wanted to know more about it.

What does it mean to be a seeker? To "seek" for something means to look for it, search for it, or try to uncover it. Whoever the Wise Men were, they began to seek God with only a little information, but great desire and honesty in their hearts. Their desire to seek and to find was so strong that they left everything behind and followed the star.

What are some other signs God uses that encourage us to seek Him? God's signs are like an artist's signature, letting everyone know who created the picture. God has placed His mark on His entire creation. "The heavens declare the glory of God" (Psalm 19:1). His surest mark is in His written word (2 Timothy 4:2), which points us to Jesus, the Word made flesh (John 1:1). God created people to know and love Him, and He draws them to Himself. He makes it clear who He is and how much He loves us in His Son, Jesus Christ.

How can we seek God? We can seek Him by listening to His Word and going to church. We can seek His forgiveness by confessing our sins and receiving His gift of grace. We can learn about God our Creator by being in His world and seeing the beauty of His artwork. It doesn't matter who you are or where you live; God will guide you to Himself as surely as He guided the Wise Men.

Sing!

What a Friend We Have in Jesus

Joseph Scriven, 1820–86

CONVERSE
Charles C. Converse, 1832–1918

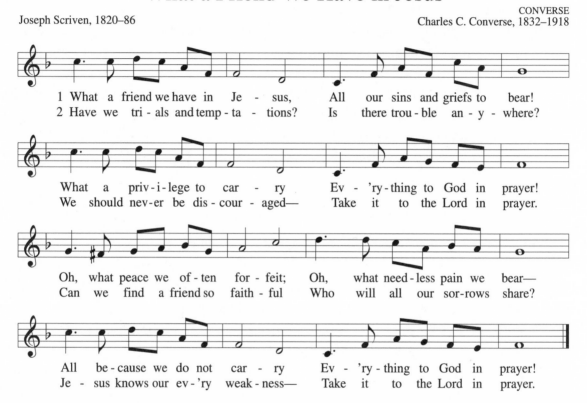

1 What a friend we have in Je - sus, All our sins and griefs to bear!
2 Have we tri - als and temp - ta - tions? Is there trou - ble an - y - where?

What a priv - i - lege to car - ry Ev - 'ry - thing to God in prayer!
We should nev - er be dis - cour - aged— Take it to the Lord in prayer.

Oh, what peace we of - ten for - feit; Oh, what need - less pain we bear—
Can we find a friend so faith - ful Who will all our sor - rows share?

All be - cause we do not car - ry Ev - 'ry - thing to God in prayer!
Je - sus knows our ev - 'ry weak - ness— Take it to the Lord in prayer.

Let's Pray

Dear God, we pray for everyone who is seeking You with a sincere heart. Direct their paths so that, through Word and Sacrament, they might find You soon. Use us to share the love of Jesus with them. Thank You for the example of the Wise Men who searched after the truth. In Jesus' name. Amen.

Nativity Building

Move the Wise Men closer. They are on their journey, following the bright star in faith, believing they will find the new king.

Day Eight of Epiphany

Lighting

Light the Christ Candle. Jesus is the Morning Star.

Reading

Revelation 22:3–5,16

Think about It

At night, far away from city lights, the moon and stars shine brightly. They have directed the paths of sailors, airplane pilots, and other night travelers throughout history and even today.

The Lord God Almighty is the Master Designer behind all of creation. Every star was created by Him. He is the One who placed that special star in the sky proclaiming Jesus' birth to all who had eyes to see. He has placed the stars in our night sky too.

Go outside and look at the night sky. Are there lots of stars? Can you find the North Star? The North Star has guided many travelers. If you are in the city, or if it's cloudy, you might not be able to see many stars; but they are there. Even one star twinkling in the sky declares the glory of God.

Have you ever seen the stars slowly fade away as the light of the morning sun bright-ens the sky? How do you think that would look? One by one the lesser light of the stars gives way to the brightness of the sun whose light takes away the darkness. It's a little like walking into a dark room and turning on the light; the darkness is overcome. Instantly. Every time.

How is Jesus like a star? Why did He call Himself "the Bright Morning Star"? His light overpowers the darkness of sin. He has taken the punishment for our sin and given us the light of God's love. Nothing is greater than the light of Jesus. In heaven, God Himself will be our light. Isn't that amazing?

How can knowing this help you the next time you are scared, or hurt, or confused? Let Jesus be your light. His light outshines even the sun. He loves you. He protects you. He lights the way to heaven for you.

Sing!

Jesus Loves Me, This I Know

Anna B. Warner, 1820–1915

William B. Bradbury, 1816–68

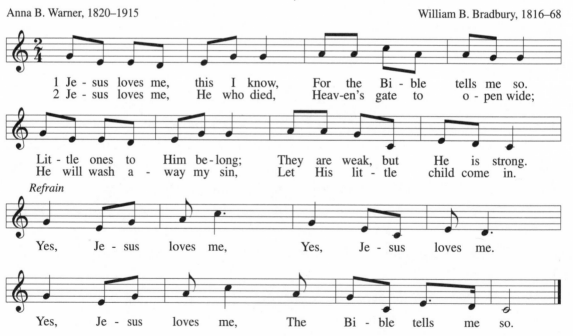

1 Je - sus loves me, this I know, For the Bi - ble tells me so.
2 Je - sus loves me, He who died, Heav-en's gate to o - pen wide;

Lit - tle ones to Him be - long; They are weak, but He is strong.
He will wash a - way my sin, Let His lit - tle child come in.

Refrain

Yes, Je - sus loves me, Yes, Je - sus loves me.

Yes, Je - sus loves me, The Bi - ble tells me so.

Let's Pray

Dear Jesus, let the light of Your love shine on us. Be our Bright Morning Star. Take away our fears with Your power to overcome the darkness. Your work is grand and glorious. We stand in awe of You. In Your name we pray. Amen.

Nativity Building

Let the star at the nativity remind you of Jesus, your Bright Morning Star.

Day Nine of Epiphany

Lighting

Light the Christ Candle. Jesus is the Son of God.

Reading

Matthew 2:1–2 and 1 Chronicles 16:8–12

Think about It

"Where is the One who has been born king of the Jews? We saw His star in the east and have come to worship Him," said the Wise Men. They left their families, their homes, and their countries for one purpose—to find the new king and worship Him. Their desire to find Jesus was overwhelming and honest. When we worship we come before God in honesty, knowing who we are—His children—and recognizing all He has done for us.

Can we worship today? Worship takes place whenever a sincere, believing heart receives God's gifts in Jesus Christ and reaches out to Him in praise for who He is. Jesus said, "God is Spirit, and His worshipers must worship in spirit and truth" (John 4:24).

Where can we worship? Worship can take place anywhere—at church, at home, in a park, at school, and even under the covers in your bed. A worship service in church is a large gathering of believers listening and responding to God together. Even your gathering as a family right now is a type of worship. Anywhere there is a heart trusting in Jesus and seeking to be closer to God through His Word, there is worship.

What is worship? How do we worship? Worship is praising God for who He is and thanking Him for what He has done. Worship is a time of reflection and response. As we gather in church within the family of faith, worship is a time to listen to God's Word, confess our sins and receive His forgiveness, sing hymns of praise, and experience God's grace through Baptism and the Lord's Supper.

Make a pledge together within the family of faith. Seek times to worship as a family at home. Take some time now to worship God together. Take turns reading the following psalms: Psalm 117; 134; 138:1–5; 147:1–5; 148; and 150. Tell each other the story of Jesus' death and resurrection. Come to God in prayer. What a mighty God we serve!

Let's Pray

Dear Lord, we worship You. We see Your goodness at work in our lives, in the lives of people in our community, in the beauty of Your creation, and in the gift of salvation. You are good. You are faithful. You have taken our sins to the cross and granted us Your forgiveness. We praise and glorify You. Amen.

Sing!

God Is So Good

Anonymous   Anonymous

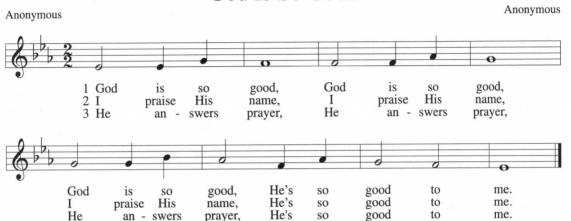

```
1 God    is    so    good,    God    is    so    good,
2 I    praise  His   name,    I    praise  His   name,
3 He    an - swers  prayer,   He    an - swers  prayer,

God    is    so    good,    He's   so   good   to   me.
I    praise  His   name,    He's   so   good   to   me.
He    an - swers  prayer,   He's   so   good   to   me.
```

Nativity Building

Move the Wise Men even closer. Their journey is almost over. Or is it? Wise men and women can still seek the Morning Star every day.

Day Ten of Epiphany

Lighting

Light the Christ Candle. Jesus is the reason we rejoice.

Reading

Matthew 18:1–5, 10–11 and John 3:16–18

119

Think about It

The Wise Men were not the only seekers. Jesus' main mission was to seek out men and women, boys and girls, and to save us from our sins. He came to restore our relationship with God the Father, and to grant us eternal life. Jesus was the first "seeker." Luke 19:10 reads, "For the Son of Man came to seek and to save what was lost."

Why did God send Jesus to earth? He sent Him to save us from our sins. There is nothing we could do to earn eternal life or pay for our own sins. Only Jesus could do that for us.

How did Jesus help people in His earthly ministry? Jesus healed people who were sick. He gave hope to people without hope. He freed people caught in sin. And He continues His ministry today among us—healing, forgiving, saving, and giving hope. We were lost in our sin and darkness until Jesus brought us back into a relationship with God the Father.

Are children important to Jesus? Yes, He loves little children. Scripture teaches that Jesus said, "Let the little children come to Me, and do not hinder them" (Matthew 19:14). In today's Bible reading, He even used a little child as an example of how everyone should believe and trust in God.

Let's Pray

Dear God, we rejoice that we have been found and that we live in the warmth of Your love. Help each of us to believe with the trust and love of a small child. We take joy in the giver of all good gifts and in Jesus Christ, His Son—the same yesterday, today, and forever. In Jesus' name. Amen.

Sing!

He's Got the Whole World in His Hands

IN HIS HANDS
American spiritual

American spiritual

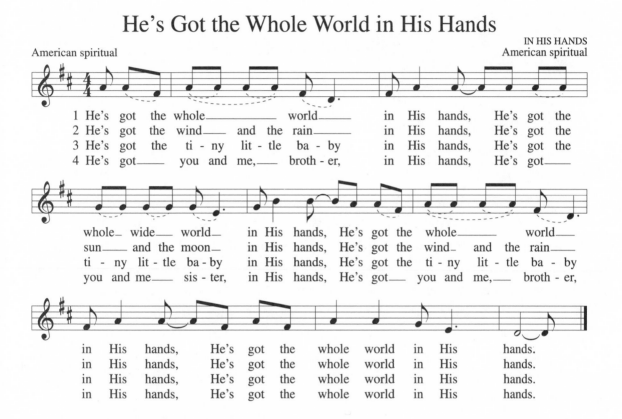

1 He's got the whole_____ world_____ in His hands, He's got the
2 He's got the wind____ and the rain_____ in His hands, He's got the
3 He's got the ti - ny lit - tle ba - by in His hands, He's got the
4 He's got____ you and me,____ broth - er, in His hands, He's got____

whole_ wide_ world_ in His hands, He's got the whole_____ world_
sun____ and the moon_ in His hands, He's got the wind_ and the rain___
ti - ny lit - tle ba - by in His hands, He's got the ti - ny lit - tle ba - by
you and me____ sis - ter, in His hands, He's got_ you and me,____ broth - er,

in His hands, He's got the whole world in His hands.
in His hands, He's got the whole world in His hands.
in His hands, He's got the whole world in His hands.
in His hands, He's got the whole world in His hands.

Nativity Building

Place a small magnifying glass next to the stable. Jesus came to seek and save the lost. We can ask Him to help us seek out those who need to hear His Good News.

121

Day Eleven of Epiphany

Lighting

Light the Christ Candle. God is always at work.

Reading

Matthew 2:7–18

Think about It

Note King Herod's reaction in today's Bible reading. No earthly king can ruin God's plans, though Herod certainly tried. He was not at all happy about the Wise Men's visit, or what they had to say. Herod responded selfishly and tried to get rid of the new king.

Was Herod aware of God's plan for this new king? At first, Herod thought about how this king would affect him and his earthly kingdom. Then he went a step further and closed his heart to God. He cut off any desire to learn about this new king; he plotted to kill Him. While Herod's plan failed to harm Jesus, he did hurt many families in Bethlehem.

Did God know what Herod was going to do? God knows everything. In Hebrews 4:13 it says, "Nothing in all creation is hidden from God's sight." He knows what goes on inside the hearts of people and He knows everything that happens because of it.

How did God protect Jesus? God sent an angel to warn Joseph in a dream. Joseph immediately obeyed and escaped to Egypt with his young family. Nothing could stop God's plan to save us; He loves us too much. God still protects His people today. Romans 8:38-39 says nothing can separate us from His love.

Do we ever try to shut God out from working in our lives? Do we ever insist on our way? If we are honest, we have to admit that sometimes we do turn away from God's plan when it is something we may not like. We may struggle against God's will at first. But even pain and disappointment will not make us close our hearts to His work if we trust in His goodness. Jesus is the King of Kings and He always desires the best for us. We can be happy, even in hard times, when we follow Jesus. His best is even better than our wildest dreams.

Sing!

My God Is So Great

Anonymous   Anonymous

My God is so great, so strong and so might-y! There's noth-ing my God can-not do! *(clap, clap)* The moun-tains are His, the riv-ers are His, the stars are His hand-i-work, too. My God is so great, so strong and so might-y! There's noth-ing my God can-not do! *(clap, clap)*

123

Let's Pray

Dear God our Father, You are so great, so strong, and so mighty. There is nothing You cannot do! We believe that You have only good plans for us—plans to help us grow in faith and love for You. Help us learn from Herod's mistake when we resist Your work in our lives. Forgive us our sins, and lead us in Your path. In Jesus' name. Amen.

Nativity Building

Place a small crown at the stable. Jesus is the King of kings. The next time something unexpected happens, look for God at work. There is nothing He cannot do for you!

Day Twelve of Epiphany

Lighting

Light the center candle first. Jesus is our Wisdom.

Reading

Matthew 7:24–29

Think about It

Imagine children on the beach spending hours working on the sandcastle. They pack the sand firmly into their molds, and carefully turn the molds upside down, setting the sand into place. They design a beautiful castle with many turrets, a bridge, and a deep moat surrounding it. Then the tide comes in.

What happens when the tide comes in? In minutes the castle will disappear under the waves. Nothing built on sand lasts for long.

How did Jesus compare the person who builds on sand with the person who builds on rock? The house that is built on sand cannot last through a rainstorm. It will fall apart. The house built on a rock has a solid foundation that can last through many storms.

Jesus went on to explain that the person building on the rock is like the person who listens to His words and puts them into practice. What about the person who built on the sand? This person is called foolish; his or her life is not built on Jesus. Their faith will not be strong enough when the problems of life come; their houses will crumble and fall. The foolish cannot stand against the storm of life without Jesus.

How can we be like the wise builder? We can listen to Jesus and seek to live our lives to His glory. When the problems of life come, we can look to Jesus for strength. In Matthew 21:42 Jesus calls Himself the capstone or cornerstone. When we build our lives on Him, we will always be strong. He is the Master Builder.

Sing!

Sing "My God Is So Great" as found on page 123.

Let's Pray

Dear Jesus, let Your wisdom guide our decisions and the plans we make for our lives. Help us to listen to You and practice what You teach. Thank You for giving us all we need to build our lives on solid ground. Strengthen us with Your love and forgiveness. In Your name we pray. Amen.

Nativity Building

The three Wise Men finally arrive! Celebrate the light of God's love in your lives today and every day!

Scripture Promises and Their Fulfillment in Jesus

Its Fulfillment	The Promise
Luke 1:32–33	Isaiah 9:7
Luke 2:4–5,7	Micah 5:2
Luke 1:26–27, 30–31	Isaiah 7:14
Matthew 2:14–15	Hosea 11:1
Matthew 3:17	Psalm 2:7
John 10:2–11	Isaiah 40:11
Luke 4:18–19	Isaiah 61:1–2
John 8:12	Isaiah 2:5
Luke 1:68–79	Genesis 2:16–17; 15:18

Acknowledgments

Unless otherwise noted the hymn texts and settings in this book are in the public domain.

CELEBRATE JESUS! AT CHRISTMAS